2108

M000011568

POLITICAL PROFILES
RUDY GIULIANI

Political Profiles
Rudy Giuliani

Anna Layton Sharp

MORGAN REYNOLDS
PUBLISHING

Greensboro, North Carolina

CHILDREN'S DEPARTMENT
KAUKAUNA PUBLIC LIBRARY

POLITICAL PROFILES

Barack Obama
Hillary Clinton
John McCain
Nancy Pelosi
Al Gore
Rudy Giuliani
Arnold Schwarzenegger

POLITICAL PROFILES: RUDY GIULIANI

Copyright © 2008 by Anna Layton Sharp

All rights reserved.
This book, or parts thereof, may not be reproduced in any form
except by written consent of the publisher. For more information write:
Morgan Reynolds Publishing, Inc., 620 South Elm Street, Suite 223
Greensboro, North Carolina 27406 USA

Library of Congress Cataloging-in-Publication Data

Sharp, Anna Layton.
  Political profiles : Rudy Giuliani / by Anna Layton Sharp.
    p. cm.
  Includes bibliographical references and index.
  ISBN-13: 978-1-59935-048-6
  ISBN-10: 1-59935-048-3
  1. Giuliani, Rudolph W. 2. Mayors--New York (State)--New York--
Biography. 3. New York (N.Y.)--Politics and government--1951- 4. New York
(N.Y.)--History--1951- 5. Presidential candidates--United States--Biography.
I. Title.
  F128.57.G58S48 2007
  974.7'1044092--dc22
  [B]

                            2007023570

Printed in the United States of America
First Edition

To Brad

Contents

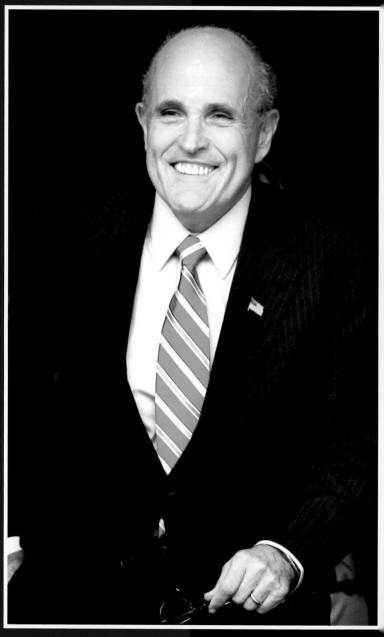

Rudy Giuliani
(Courtesy of AP Images/Rob Carr)

one
Yankee Fan

*T*uesday, September 11, 2001, was the primary election day in New York City. Mayor Rudy Giuliani could not run for a third term. Restricted by term limits, he had only four more months in office. "I'm never going to have a better job," he had announced at his final State of the City address.

The last months had been difficult. His second marriage had ended in a very messy, public divorce, he was diagnosed with prostate cancer, and his approval rating had sunk to 37 percent, an all-time low. In May 2000 he bowed out of the New York Senate race, which would have pitted him against First Lady Hillary Clinton.

On the morning of 9/11, Giuliani was a lame-duck mayor having breakfast at the Peninsula hotel on 55th street, a few miles from the twin towers of World Trade Center, located in the financial district in lower Manhattan.

Shortly before nine o'clock in the morning, as primary voters began arriving at the polls to nominate his successor, Giuliani received a call. A plane had flown into the North Tower of the World Trade Center. Looking up at the clear blue sky, the mayor had to assume that the crash was deliberate. Any pilot would have been able to avoid the 1,776 foot tower. Immediately, he and his aides climbed into his black Chevrolet Suburban and made a beeline for the area that would soon come to be known as Ground Zero. He arrived minutes after a second plane hit the South Tower at 9:03.

The terrorist attacks of September 11, 2001, occurred at the end of Giuliani's terms as mayor of New York. *(Courtesy of FEMA)*

After the second plane hit, it was clear that New York was under terrorist attack. Giuliani's administration had tried to prepare for such an attack. In 1996, Giuliani built a state-of-the-art Emergency Command Center that contained stockpiles of antidotes and medical treatments, a high-tech communication system, and a generator in case of power failure. The only problem was its location: the 23rd floor of Seven World Trade Center, a building just north of the Twin Towers. When Giuliani arrived, the building was being evacuated. He and his team went in search of an office space they could use as a temporary command post. They found one right around the corner at 75 Barclay Street.

Giuliani had just commandeered a cubicle and gotten Vice President Dick Cheney on the phone when the line went dead. Seconds later, there was a thunderous roar. One block away, the South Tower had collapsed. The ground quaked from the avalanche of a half of a million tons of concrete, steel, and glass. The temporary command post filled with smoke and debris, and rubble piled outside the building's exits, blocking any routes of escape. Mayor Giuliani was trapped inside.

***

Giuliani's childhood taught him how to remain calm in the face of adversity. Raised a New York Yankees fan in the shadow of Ebbets field, the home of the Brooklyn Dodgers, Rudolph "Rudy" Giuliani was a favorite target of neighborhood bullies. "If you can survive as a Yankee fan in Brooklyn, you can survive anything, anywhere, by anyone," says a former Giuliani adviser.

Giuliani's parents, both children of Italian immigrants, were native New Yorkers. Harold, born in Manhattan, was a lifelong Yankees fan, a loyalty he would pass on to his son

Giuliani's childhood home was close to Ebbets Field, the home stadium for the former Brooklyn Dodgers, which now reside in Los Angeles. *(Courtesy of AP Images)*

Rudy. He met Brooklyn-born Helen D'Avanzo at the onset of the Great Depression. During their seven-year courtship, Harold lacked steady employment and the couple went on picnics in the park, took evening strolls, and occasionally splurged on a movie—tickets were only thirty-five cents.

Helen's brothers didn't approve of Harold, who they considered a hot-headed troublemaker. He had dropped out of high school and was arrested for burglary as a teenager, and was known for his quick temper.

Helen was as shy as Harold was outgoing and aggressive. One of the best students in her class, she skipped two grades and graduated high school at the age of sixteen. Her dream was to become a teacher, but financial hardships kept her from attending college. Her father had died when she was fifteen, and after high school she went to work to help support her mother and six siblings.

Harold, on the other hand, had trouble holding a job. He got into so many street fights—one right in front of Helen when he felt her honor had been offended—that he started signing his love letters to her "your savage."

Soon after his twenty-sixth birthday, Harold proved he deserved the nickname. On April 2, 1934, he robbed a milkman at gunpoint. At his arraignment he lied about his name, age, and address and pled not guilty to the four felony charges. At the hearing in May, he changed his mind and pled guilty to lesser charges. The judge sentenced him to two to five years in Sing Sing State Prison. After serving a year and a half, he was paroled.

In 1936 Harold and Helen were married, but Harold didn't settle down overnight. He took a job tending bar at his brother-in-law Leo D'Avanzo's restaurant. D'Avanzo was the black sheep of Helen's family. His restaurant, Vincent's, was a known hangout for members of the Italian Mafia. D'Avanzo and his business partner, Jimmy Dano, ran a loan-sharking operation out of Vincent's, loaning money to people illegally and charging them exorbitant interest rates. Interest and commissions began at 150 percent and rose each week. It was a profitable criminal enterprise, and the restaurant had a secret room in the back for handling all the cash. Customers would pay at the bar, passing envelopes to Harold across the counter. Sometimes he collected as much as $15,000 a week.

Those who missed a payment had to deal with Harold's notorious temper. As D'Avanzo's enforcer, he was the muscle behind the operation. Harold used threats or violence to make sure people paid their debts. He broke noses, smashed kneecaps, and hit at least one man across the face with a baseball bat.

Even though debtors feared Harold, to his relatives he was an affectionate man. They knew him for his warm hugs, contagious enthusiasm (especially when talking politics), and sparkling gray eyes. He didn't want to work as an enforcer for his brother-in-law forever, especially after he and Helen had children. They longed for a family of their own, but year after year were disappointed. When the couple's first and only child was finally born, on May 28, 1944, they thought of him as a miracle baby and an answer to their prayers. They named him Rudolph William Louis Giuliani III, after his paternal grandfather Rodolpho who had immigrated to the U.S. from Montecatini, Italy, in 1899.

Helen never lost her passion for teaching, and Rudy became his mother's star—and only—pupil. "Instead of a class to teach, she made me her special student," he says. She read to him from history books and biographies when he was just a toddler. Rudy grew up discussing current events with his parents. Helen, a Republican, and Harold, a Democrat, enjoyed watching political conventions. Like most of America, they followed the Kefauver hearings, a televised investigation of organized crime broadcast in 1950 and 1951. Helen would continue to inspire her son's interest in government well into his adolescence and adulthood. As a teenager, Rudy sometimes found politics more interesting than girls. A high school friend remembers that he and Rudy once abandoned

Giuliani's mother, Helen, inspired his interest in politics. This photo shows Helen *(far right)* with Giuliani and his wife and son during his 1989 New York mayoral candidacy announcement. *(Courtesy of AP Images/ Mario Suriani)*

their dates in the living room while they discussed politics in the kitchen with Mrs. Giuliani.

Rudy's father fought to make sure his son didn't end up on the wrong side of the law as he had. He never missed an opportunity to teach young Rudy the value of hard work and honesty. Until Wayne Barrett investigated Harold's criminal past and published his findings in 2000, Giuliani claims he didn't realize the full extent of his father's checkered past. "I knew parts of it, but it was always a big secret and very shadowy. I knew he had gotten into trouble as a young man, but I never knew exactly what it was," he said.

> My father compensated through me. In a very exaggerated way, he made sure that I didn't repeat his mistakes in my life— which I thank him for, because it worked out. . . . He would say over and over, 'You can't take anything that's not yours. You can't steal. Never lie, never steal.' As a child and even as a young adult, I thought, What does he keep doing this for? I'm not going to steal anything.

Two of Giuliani's closest childhood friends, Alan Placa and Peter Powers, both say they were unaware of Giuliani's father's history. "His parents brought him up with strong values," says Powers.

One lesson Harold taught his son was the importance of supporting the government. He prepared tax returns for relatives, sometimes working until three or four in the morning. When Rudy would ask him if he hated it, his father would lecture him. "It's a great privilege to pay your taxes," he would tell his son. "Just think of all those people who would like to come to America just to have the privilege to pay taxes. Better pay every single penny of them."

Harold, however reformed, still wanted his son to develop street smarts. He gave Rudy boxing gloves when he was only two years old. The two would spend hours in the basement going over Rudy's technique. When Helen would ask her husband to discipline their son, Harold would take Rudy downstairs and pretend to spank him. She didn't know that they actually used the time to practice boxing.

The pint-sized Yankee fan would need to learn to defend himself—dressed in the team's famous pinstriped uniform, he was a visible target. "As a Yankees fan growing up only blocks from Ebbets Field in Brooklyn—home to the Dodgers—I soon discovered that those lessons came in handy," Giuliani later recalled. Harold taught his son how to throw punches, but he was sure to tell Rudy not to pick on someone smaller. "Never be a bully," Giuliani remembers hearing repeatedly. Years later, people critical of the mayor's intimidating administrative style would say that this particular piece of fatherly advice went in one ear and out the other.

Rudy's baseball allegiance wasn't the only reason he got roughed up on the streets of Brooklyn. He was small for his age, with a pale complexion and a nervous tic in one eye. When he was five years old, the kids in his neighborhood tried to hang him from a tree, not understanding that they could have killed him. "New York produces tough kids; tough kids become tough adults," says a Giuliani aide.

Rudy got a change of scenery when he was seven. Like many families in the 1950s, the Giulianis decided to move to the suburbs. Their modest, brick-faced house was located in an orderly housing development on a tree-lined street paved with bluestone pebbles. The small community of Garden City South on Long Island was much less racially diverse than their old inner-city neighborhood, but the Giulianis were not searching for an all-white cocoon—they were trying to protect their son from the influence of members of their own family. Harold told a friend he was moving to get away from his in-laws.

Harold didn't want Rudy exposed to his brother-in-law Leo, or Leo's son Lewis. Lewis hung around his dad's bar all day, and Harold saw trouble in his nephew's future. He was right. Lewis grew up to become a mob associate and to run a stolen car ring. He racked up a long criminal record and became a suspect in several homicides. In 1977, he was shot to death by F.B.I. agents when he tried to run them over with his car.

Unlike his mob-connected family members in Brooklyn, Rudy's relatives on Long Island included role models like firefighters and policemen. "I grew up with uniforms all around me and their stories of heroism," he says.

In Long Island, Rudy attended a local Catholic school, St. Anne's, where he was a top student. After passing a rigorous test his final year, he was one of two students handpicked by his parish to attend the prestigious, all-male Bishop Loughlin Memorial High School in Brooklyn. For the next four years, Rudy made the tedious commute. He took the Long Island Rail Road to Penn Station, where he caught the No. 1 subway. Loughlin, at 242nd Street, was the last stop on the line.

Scholarship students made up most of Loughlin's student body and nearly all of its graduates went on to college. It provided kids from working-class families with the chance to get a first-class education.

Rudy was intelligent, but he didn't make the best grades and had a reputation as a cutup. On a class trip to Washington, D.C., he and a few friends started a water fight in the hotel that soaked the carpets. The furious manager gave them ten minutes to pack their bags and get downstairs. His classmates were panic-stricken and sure they'd face expulsion, but Rudy called the manager's bluff. Instead of packing, he went to sleep. "Rudy was right," remembers Peter Powers. "[He had an] incredible ability to assess a situation."

While many of his classmates recall Giuliani's quick wit and sense of humor, others remember him as being an "oddball." He was chubby and had a lisp, and he was such an opera buff that he founded a school opera club. Since his father preferred boxing and baseball to opera, Rudy would usually hole up in his room and listen to his records alone. Rudy's grandfather

While attending Bishop Loughlin Memorial High School, Giuliani organized trips for students to see performances by the Metropolitan Opera.

Rodolpho had loved opera, too—but unlike Rudy, he didn't play his records in private. Rodolpho turned up the volume as loud as it would go and sang along . . . which makes it easy to guess where Harold got his aversion.

Rudy and Peter wanted to share their love of opera with their classmates, so they organized trips for students to see performances by the Metropolitan Opera in Manhattan and the Brooklyn Academy of Music. For $1.50 they could stand in the balcony. "Whatever he got into, he put his heart and soul into it," says Brother Peter Bonventre, the school's assistant principal. One student remembers Giuliani's flair for leadership. "Giuliani was always around, always leading something, always looking ahead," he says.

Rudy's interests went beyond opera. He also showed an interest in politics and government service. Fascinated with the

presidential election of 1960, he supported Democratic candidate John F. Kennedy, who would become the country's first
Catholic president. Once Rudy played hooky to see Kennedy
give a talk in Queens. Rudy considered himself a Democrat,
like his father, and he would support the Democratic Party
for years before becoming a Republican.

Despite his interest in national politics, Rudy never ran
for student office in high school. Instead, he worked as a
campaign manager for his friend George, who was running
for student council president. Rudy demonstrated charisma

Giuliani became enthralled with the presidential election of 1960, in
which he favored Democratic candidate John F. Kennedy.

and a natural ability for glad-handing. Although his candidate didn't win, the next year the senior class voted Rudy "class politician."

Throughout his childhood and adolescence, Rudy spent time with his extended family. During the summer, his paternal grandmother rented a small cliffside cottage overlooking the Long Island Sound. Rudy's aunts, uncles, and cousins would all squeeze together on the weekends. At dinnertime, the dining table could be hauled into the driveway to seat up to twenty-five. Over large plates of pasta, the adults would talk politics. As a teen, Rudy joined the discussion, debating with his relatives about civil rights and Soviet Russia. Sleeping arrangements were part of the adventure—almost everyone had to find a place on the floor; a lucky few got mattresses or box springs.

Up the road from the Giuliani cottage, Rudy's second cousin Regina Peruggi—her father was Harold's first cousin—had a summer house with her family. The Peruggis, who lived in the Bronx, would sometimes join the Giuliani clan for weekend theme parties. On Roman night everyone dressed in togas; for the luau there were floral shirts and homemade leis. One Saturday night Regina taught her cousins how to dance "the funky chicken," a group dance popular in the 1950s and '60s.

Regina had more in common with her older cousin Rudy than just kinship. She also came from a middle-class background—her father was an RCA Victor record salesman, and her mother was a former Rockette. Like Rudy she was politically passionate and admired John F. Kennedy.

One summer, Rudy brought a girlfriend out to the beach. She remembers an attraction between her boyfriend and

Giuliani's first wife, Regina Peruggi

Regina. "I think she had a crush on Rudy," she says. "I knew she had a crush on him. Isn't that funny?" The girlfriend's instincts were right on—Rudy and Regina would get married in 1968.

But as a high school student, Rudy wasn't sure if he would ever marry—he considered becoming a priest. He signed up his senior year to enter a religious order devoted to missionary work, and many of his classmates wrote "Good luck in seminary" in his yearbook. According to one of his teachers, Rudy had to put his plans for the priesthood on hold when his father became sick. Harold was experiencing heart problems and ulcers. In his best-selling memoir, *Leadership*, Giuliani admits a different motive for his change of plans. "I realized I had a problem: my budding interest in the opposite sex was something that wouldn't be suppressed." Giuliani enrolled in Manhattan College in Riverdale, The Bronx, hoping that he'd be ready for celibacy after a year or two.

He wasn't. Giuliani enjoyed dating and decided that the priesthood wasn't for him after all. His parents were not disappointed by his choice. "The Giulianis wanted grandchildren," says a family neighbor. One of Giuliani's most serious college girlfriends was Kathy Livermore, a tall, attractive blonde. The two met over the summer while working at the same bank—Giuliani was an assistant and Livermore a teller. On one of their dates, Giuliani got angry when another guy made a crude remark to Livermore, and he did just what his father would have done . . . he punched the guy in the face.

Having ruled out a future in the clergy, Giuliani decided he'd become a surgeon. He enrolled in his school's premed program. For his first year, Giuliani received four A's, three B's and one C. The C was in an art class.

Giuliani didn't take too many premed classes before realizing that his love of debate was pointing him toward a different calling—the law. Taking courses in United States history, he developed an interest in Western civilization. Learning about democracy and the ideal of equal opportunity reinforced the principles that his father had taught him to value at a young age. The school's course load was heavy, but Giuliani found time to write a liberal column for *Quadrangle*, the student newspaper. His sophomore year, he and his old friend Peter Powers ran for student council—Giuliani for president and Powers for treasurer. They campaigned together, standing outside classrooms shaking hands and passing out buttons. Their effort paid off—both Giuliani and Powers won. It was Giuliani's first electoral victory.

Fired up by his success, Giuliani decided to pledge the most selective fraternity on campus. For weeks he submitted himself to hazing—shining the brothers' shoes, eating raw eggs and bowls of garlic, and getting hit on the backside with a wooden paddle.

After all that, Giuliani didn't make the cut. They blackballed him the first vote. He was humiliated but he didn't feel sorry for himself for long. He decided to pledge a little-known fraternity and take over as its president. With the help of his best friends Peter and Alan, he increased membership from five to thirty.

As an upperclassman, Giuliani got involved in national politics, working on Robert F. Kennedy's campaign for the U.S. Senate. Most important, Giuliani took his own shot at public office. In 1964, at age twenty-one, he was elected Democratic district leader in Nassau County. He practiced his political speeches for Kathy, asking her to critique different hand gestures. The two of them discussed politics frequently, and one day Giuliani told her his greatest aspiration: "to be the first Italian American President of the United States."

After graduating with a major in political science and philosophy, Giuliani enrolled in the New York University School of Law in Manhattan. He lived with his parents on and off over the next three years, in the split-level home in

North Bellmore they had moved to several years earlier. Neighbors remember seeing a light on in his room late into the night. He would study until one or two o'clock, and then get up a five in the morning. He would keep similar hours throughout his career.

But it wasn't all work and no play. After he and Kathy broke up, Giuliani found love with his childhood friend and second cousin Regina Peruggi. While he was a student at Manhattan College, Regina was living at home and commuting to the College of New Rochelle. She majored in sociology and graduated in 1967.

Years earlier Giuliani had taken Regina to his high school junior prom. Their fathers, first cousins, drove them to the dance and then picked them afterward. The foursome had dinner at a Brooklyn restaurant. "Quite a family affair!" Regina recalls.

Away from parental chaperones, while Giuliani finished law school and Regina worked as a drug abuse counselor, their relationship grew more serious. Giuliani's mother didn't approve—but not because they were cousins. She thought their personalities were incompatible. "My son is very affectionate, he's always hugging and kissing," she explained. "Gina is lovely, but is very quiet and shy." Over Helen's objections, Giuliani proposed and Regina accepted.

In 1968, Giuliani graduated with honors. In October of the same year, he and Regina were married in a Catholic ceremony at Regina's church, St. Philip Neri in the Bronx.

two
Crime Buster

After he graduated from law school, Giuliani wanted to work as a judge's clerk. The clerkship would teach him the ins and outs of being a trial lawyer, but it wouldn't pay as well as a job at a private law firm. When Giuliani started as a junior clerk, his salary was $6,900. Two years later, he was making $11,000. "I thought I was rich," he says.

Clerking jobs were very competitive and usually went to students from the Ivy League schools—like Giuliani's hero John F. Kennedy, who studied at Harvard. Judge Lloyd MacMahon in the Southern District of New York cared more about street smarts than pedigree, and he was impressed by Giuliani's ambition and dedication.

Judge MacMahon was a tough, demanding boss, but was also a committed teacher to his clerks. Giuliani says his clerkship experience changed his life forever. Throughout his career he would value the Judge's friendship and ask his advice before making major professional decisions. He also credits Judge MacMahon with inspiring him toward public office. "It wasn't until I understood how effective a leader Judge MacMahon was—and how he got those who worked for him to believe in themselves and accomplish more than they thought they could—that I started to think I might be capable of similar responsibilities."

Judge MacMahon even helped Giuliani avoid military service in Vietnam. Giuliani had already received several student deferments, but as a law clerk his application was rejected. Judge MacMahon wrote a letter to the draft board on Giuliani's behalf. The rare occupational deferment Judge MacMahon helped Giuliani receive may come back to haunt him in the 2008 presidential election. "If Giuliani is the nominee, we're going to hammer him with ads, and it's going to be easy because the issue is simple: He's a draft dodger," says Jon Soltz, an Iraq veteran who runs VoteVets.org, a political action committee that supports Democratic candidates.

Giuliani's deferment expired in 1970, but he was never drafted. He insists that if he had been called up, he would have served.

As his time under Judge MacMahon's wing came to an end, Giuliani felt confident in his knowledge of the law and the career prospects before him. "There's a big gap, though, between that and the real world," he says. But with the prestigious clerkship under his belt, Giuliani's future was bright.

As Giuliani started his law career in the real world, a decade of the Cultural Revolution was coming to an end. The 1960s had seen the Beatles come to America, the first man walk on the moon, and the assassination of civil rights leader Reverend Martin Luther King, Jr., and Senator Robert

In July 1969, Neil Armstrong was the first man to walk on the moon.
(Courtesy of NASA)

F. Kennedy. There had also been massive protests against American involvement in the war in Vietnam, and an increase in illegal drug use.

In 1970, Giuliani became a prosecutor in the office of the U.S. Attorney for the Southern District of New York, one of the offices that represents the United States federal government. His job was to argue the government's side in court cases tried in New York City and the surrounding area. The Southern District has a reputation for attracting the best and the brightest, and Giuliani likes to compare it to the Yankees. "The U.S. Attorney's office in the Southern District of New York is the preeminent prosecutor's office in the country," he

In 1970, Giuliani began working as a prosecutor in the office of the U.S. Attorney for the Southern District of New York. *(Courtesy of AP Images)*

says. Just like big shot baseball players, the young attorneys there "think they're always right."

Giuliani was only twenty-six years old when he started working as a trial lawyer in the Southern District, but he already had his eye on the top position in the office. "I tried the most difficult case rather than the easier ones, not only because I believed in my abilities as a prosecutor but because

I knew it would help me run the U.S. Attorney's Office," he says. His quickly rose to the top. In three years, Giuliani became Chief of the Narcotics Unit, responsible for investigating and prosecuting major drug traffickers. He earned a reputation as a master of cross-examination.

In 1983 Giuliani would reach his ultimate goal, becoming an executive U.S. attorney and running the Southern District office. But first his career would take him to Washington, D.C.

In 1975 Harold Tyler, a former Southern District judge, hired Giuliani as associate deputy attorney general in the United States Department of Justice. "I didn't even know what the job was," Giuliani says, "but I knew it would be an opportunity to see at a relatively high level how the federal government operated." It was the first time Giuliani had lived out of the New York City area, and it would be an important catalyst in his transformation into politics. Tyler taught Giuliani a valuable lesson about leadership. "Tyler was very good under pressure," Giuliani says. "I learned from him that in a pressure situation, the best thing to do was to remain calmer than everybody else. I also learned that it was good to become angry and upset when everybody else is calm and complacent. It helps to motivate them."

While at the Justice Department, Giuliani was focused on the job at hand and didn't have much time to spend planning a future in politics. Richard Thornburgh, a colleague of Giuliani's at the Justice Department who went on to become governor of Pennsylvania, says he and Giuliani talked frequently, but political aspirations weren't a focus of their conversation. He and the others in the Justice Department expected great things from Giuliani, but they didn't know what road he would take. "We expected that Rudy would have a meaningful career, whether it was in politics or within the Justice Department or as a judge," Thornburgh says.

Giuliani had started his job during a challenging time. The U.S. Senate was formally investigating illegal activities within the government. These hearings, called the Church

Giuliani started working for the Department of Justice at the height of the Watergate scandal investigation, which eventually led to the resignation of President Nixon.

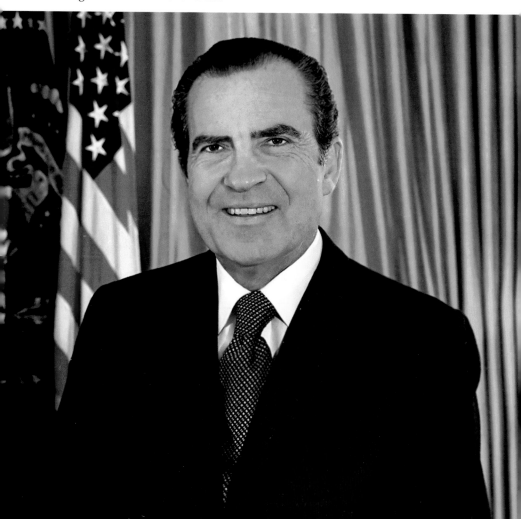

Committee hearings, were a direct response to the Watergate scandal. "Watergate" refers to the Watergate Hotel in Washington, D.C. where the Democratic National Committee was headquartered in 1972. Members of President Richard Nixon's administration hired five men—including former CIA operatives—to break into the Democratic headquarters and plant listening devices. The administration then tried to cover up their illegal activity, which only made things worse. President Nixon eventually resigned and several of his aides went to jail.

It was two newspaper journalists that brought the scandal to light. Their investigation ushered in a new era of aggressive reporting. One effect of the new investigative era was that politicians' personal conduct was no longer off-limits to reporters.

The Church Committee hearings also changed how government intelligence agencies collect information. Because President Nixon had ordered secret wiretaps of people who were opposed to his policies, there was a strong feeling in the nation that the power of the federal government to spy on citizens' lives should be curtailed. The Senate investigators found that the CIA (Central Intelligence Agency) had broken the law by opening mail and recording telephone conversations, and the Committee changed the law to protect Americans' privacy. Many of these reforms also applied to the Justice Department.

Giuliani's responsibility during his time in Washington, during the administration of President Gerald Ford, was in the area of white-collar crime. White-collar crimes are nonviolent crimes committed for financial gain, like fraud and insider trading. Giuliani also handled cases involving

While working in the Republican administration of President Ford, Giuliani came to respect and embrace the Republican party.

tax evasion—a crime his patriotic dad had found especially disgraceful.

Up to this point, the heroes in Giuliani's life had all been Democrats—including his father and President John F. Kennedy. But now he was working in the Republican administration of President Gerald Ford and meeting lots of powerful people in the Republican Party. These relationships challenged his ideas about the Republican Party. "The image I had of Republicans, as morally inferior to Democrats, came from being a prejudiced New Yorker,"

By 1975, Giuliani was working as an associate deputy attorney general in the United States Department of Justice. *(Courtesy of AP Images/Dennis Cook)*

he says. He was surprised to learn that "Lo! They did care for people."

Up to this point, Giuliani hadn't wanted to join the Republican Party because he thought they were perceived as less sensitive to the poor and working class. He had always identified with the working-class people he had grown up with in Brooklyn and Long Island. But in Washington, D.C., after getting to know leaders in both parties, Giuliani had to acknowledge that his beliefs were more in line with the

Republican Party. In 1976, he changed his voter registration to Republican, and, for the first time, he voted for a Republican candidate for president.

After Giuliani's second year in Washington, Republicans lost power when Democrat Jimmy Carter won the presidency. Giuliani's boss, Harold Tyler, brought him back to New York and made him partner at his firm Patterson, Belknap, Webb & Tyler. This was Giuliani's first experience in private law.

Giuliani didn't have time to get comfortable in private practice. He returned to public service in 1981 after the inauguration of Republican President Ronald Reagan. The new president nominated him as associate attorney general in the U.S. Department of Justice, the Department's third most senior position. Giuliani was thirty, the youngest associate attorney general in U.S. history.

Even though his career was taking off, Giuliani's marriage was at a dead end. Years of long work hours had taken its toll. In 1982, after fourteen years of marriage, he filed for legal separation and he and Regina were divorced within months. The end of his marriage wasn't the only personal difficulty Giuliani was facing. His father had recently died of prostate cancer at age seventy-three.

Giuliani began dating a woman named Donna Hanover. As associate attorney general, Giuliani frequently traveled to Miami for business. Giuliani was the man in charge and, at times, the spokesperson for the Reagan Administration's war on drugs. In one television appearance he had been interviewed by Donna Hanover, who worked as a television journalist. After the interview, the two went to dinner at Joe's Stone Crab in Miami Beach. Weeks later Giuliani proposed at Disneyworld.

As the couple planned their wedding, Giuliani had more on his mind than guest lists and honeymoon destinations. Even though he had received a legal divorce from Regina, he wanted an annulment from the Catholic Church—a declaration that his first marriage was not valid and therefore null and void. Giuliani's argument was that he hadn't known that he and Regina were so closely related. Regina was offended and protested, but Giuliani's friend since childhood Alan Placa, a high-ranking official in the church, helped get the annulment approved.

Giuliani's motives for seeking the annulment aren't clear. Catholics who divorce and remarry can't receive Holy Communion, but he and Donna weren't regular churchgoers.

Giuliani stands with his second wife, Donna Hanover, in this 1989 photo. *(Courtesy of AP Images/Gerald Herbert)*

It's possible that Giuliani had political reasons. Voters tend to frown on divorce, and only one U.S. president has been divorced.

In April 1984, Giuliani and Donna were married in a Catholic ceremony at St. Monica's Church in Manhattan. The couple would later have two children—Andrew was born in 1986, and Caroline, born in 1989.

Giuliani's time with the Department of Justice and his life in Washington came to an end when President Reagan nominated him as an executive U.S. Attorney in the Southern District of New York in 1983. It was the job Giuliani had wanted since he was a young assistant prosecutor. Giuliani's old boss and mentor Judge MacMahon administered the oath of office.

Just as Giuliani had been the youngest associate attorney general, he was also the youngest man to lead the Southern District, an office of more than one hundred of the country's top attorneys. Giuliani's return to the Southern District meant a pay cut, but it was not a step down. "Being the U.S. Attorney was the best," says a former Giuliani colleague. "That's where the action is." Nostalgia also motivated Giuliani—he missed fighting crime in his hometown. He devoted long hours—even working on the weekends—to his job. Most days he wouldn't get home until after midnight.

The new position also made Giuliani famous in New York and around the country for prosecuting members of the mafia, and inside traders on Wall Street. He also jailed drug dealers and fought government corruption.

Giuliani's success as a prosecutor meant a lot to him on a personal level. The first Italian American to be United States Attorney in the Southern District in New York, he hoped his

In 1983, President Reagan nominated Giuliani as an executive U.S. attorney for the Southern District of New York. *(Courtesy of AP Images/ Richard Drew)*

position would help break down negative stereotypes. For decades, the Italian Mafia had been a plague on New York. "I think the fact that he was of Italian heritage himself made him a tough prosecutor; he wanted to bend over backwards to root out and successfully prosecute organized crime," says a

New York attorney. "He felt that Italian Americans suffered unfairly by gangsters being Italian and he resented it."

One of Giuliani's achievements as U.S. Attorney was restoring people's confidence in the government's ability fight the mob. "It's about time law enforcement got as organized as organized crime," he told reporters.

Giuliani was also skillful at handling the press. He welcomed media coverage, and used talk shows, panel discussions, and other outlets to bring attention to his cases. He hoped the publicity would serve as a deterrent. "I want to send a message," he explained.

Of course, being in the spotlight also helped Giuliani's future in politics. The day after he arrested fifty mafia leaders, Giuliani appeared on two national evening newscasts. The following morning he appeared on *Good Morning America*. An assistant in his office told the *National Law Journal*, "A lot of people around here feel as if they're being used to launch somebody's political career."

Giuliani also received media attention by becoming an expert in white-collar crime. Giuliani wanted to show that illegal activity would not be tolerated, whether the criminal was a drug dealer on the street or a man in a suit and tie.

Insider trading was a big problem in the 1980s. Corrupt stockbrokers broke the law, making money by trading with information not available to the public. In 1987, Giuliani targeted a financial executive at Goldman Sachs—one of the world's largest and most respected investment banking firms. U.S. Marshals arrested Robert Freeman in front of his colleagues, pushing him against the wall, frisking him, and putting him in handcuffs before leading him away in tears. Freeman was ultimately cleared of all charges, and people criticized Giuliani for using excessive force. He defended the arrest, saying that just because white-collar criminals were rich and powerful didn't mean they deserved special treatment. "This isn't an invitation to a tea party," he told a *Vanity Fair* reporter.

One of the most notorious white-collar criminals Giuliani prosecuted was Leona Helmsley, a wealthy hotel operator. She once told her maid, "Only the little people pay taxes." She was convicted of cheating the government out of $1.2 million in federal income taxes, and she served eighteen months in prison.

Giuliani gained notoriety by prosecuting high-profile white-collar cases such as the one against Leona Helmsley, a wealthy hotel operator, for tax evasion. *(Courtesy of AP Images/David Cantor)*

The U.S. Attorney's Office didn't look the other way when city officials broke the law. Government corruption was widespread, and Giuliani was determined to set himself apart from all the scandal. "In a tarnished, soulless city, he was Mr. Clean," says biographer Wayne Barrett.

Between 1985 and 1988, one hundred city employees were convicted of bribery and fraud, and many more were kicked out of office. Giuliani, as a future Republican candidate, benefited immensely from these cases. By exposing corruption within New York's mostly Democratic government, he opened the door to the possibility of a Republican mayor.

During his time as U.S. Attorney, Giuliani continued to work nights and weekends. But other people worked hard, too, and they resented him for always taking center stage. "Every time the F.B.I., whose people really did the grunt work, brought in a case with a big bow on it, he would insist on taking the lead," says a former Giuliani aide. "If anyone else held a press conference, he'd go nuts. *Nuts.* The man does not do a duet, he only does a solo."

Those who got tired of seeing Giuliani's picture in the paper couldn't argue with his performance. As U.S. attorney he rarely lost. With 4,152 convictions and only twenty-five reversals, his remains one of the best records ever.

three
The Giuliani Revolution

Despite Giuliani's efforts, the streets of New York City weren't free of crime when he resigned as U.S. attorney in 1989. He knew that as mayor he could do even more to help the city he loved. His reputation as a crime buster would be the foundation of his campaign.

Some people considered Giuliani's transition into politics inevitable. One prominent Republican lawyer called him "a candidate in search of an office." He had briefly considered running for the U.S. Senate, but he soon abandoned the idea—or at least put it on hold.

After leaving the U.S. Attorney's Office when the Reagan administration ended, Giuliani reentered private practice and began planning to run for mayor of New York City. A week before his forty-fifth birthday, he announced his candidacy.

He wrote his speech on a yellow legal pad, the same kind he'd used as a student at Bishop Loughlin. He went back to his high school to deliver the speech. "This is the city of my

By 1990, New York had become a city filled with crime, poverty, and homelessness. *(Courtesy of AP Images/Marty Lederhandler)*

roots," he announced. "All of my past draws me to take on this challenge, to restore the city of my grandparents and parents, of my relatives and my friends and to offer hope to New Yorkers once again."

At the time, New Yorkers were short on hope. For years mental hospitals had been releasing more and more patients, many of whom ended up living on the streets. Crack cocaine use was an epidemic in inner cities across the country. Almost a million people in New York City were on welfare—the highest number since the Great Depression. The city, once home to 131 Fortune 500 companies, had seen more than one hundred of them leave by 1990. One survey revealed that 59 percent of New Yorkers wished they could leave, too.

Times Square, one of the world's most famous intersections and a symbol of New York, was rundown. Addicts openly bought and sold drugs, and sex shops lined the street. Muggings were common, and "squeegee men" greeted drivers as they came out of Lincoln Tunnel, demanding money in exchange for cleaning car windshields. Aggressive panhandling might not have been a major crime, but it hurt New Yorkers' quality of life and the image of the city.

Giuliani experienced the city's unruliness firsthand. Once, on his way to the theater with friends, he saw a mugger being chased by two tourists. Giuliani caught up with the tourists, an older married couple, but the thief was long gone. He had snatched the woman's purse and shoved her to the sidewalk. She was shaken up and crying. Giuliani called 911 and searched the area for a police officer. There were none

In 1989, Giuliani decided to run for mayor of New York City. *(Courtesy of AP Images/Gerald Herbert)*

around. Fifteen minutes went by and still no cops appeared. Giuliani knew that in order to make New York a good place to live, work, and visit, the city's leaders had to do a better job making people feel safe and protected. "As I waited for the police," he says, "I thought, 'This has got to change.'"

With the city falling apart, voters liked the idea of a "tough cop" mayor to clean up the streets. Giuliani's background in law enforcement made him a natural choice. A reporter for *The New York Times* said that Giuliani came across as "a crusading Batman to New York City's gritty Gotham."

The race for mayor was close, but Giuliani lost to Democrat David Dinkins by two percentage points, or about 40,000 votes out of 2 million cast. It was the closest election in the city's history and a strong performance for a first-time candidate, especially a Republican. The city hadn't elected a Republican mayor in more than twenty years.

Giuliani's late start in the race hurt his campaign, and he would have had a better chance of winning if the Conservative Party of New York, a minor but influential party, had backed him. Instead, they gave their support to a man named Ronald Lauder, the wealthy son of cosmetics mogul Estée Lauder. Giuliani had to run as a "fusion" candidate for both the Republican Party and the Liberal party, another minor third party active in New York. Poor organization also contributed to Giuliani's loss. Most of the people working on his campaign were his friends, and didn't have much experience in politics.

On top of everything else, Giuliani wasn't the most polished candidate. Early in his political career, some critics described his appearance as "wooden" and "robotic." He once dropped in on a stickball game in Harlem wearing a suit. Tabloids ran

During Giuliani's first campaign for mayor, he was described as "wooden" and "robotic." In this photo, he is attempting to pass a football in his suit and tie. *(Courtesy of AP Images/Mark D. Phillips)*

photos of him swinging at a pitch while wearing a jacket and tie. His public speaking skills were more suited to a court-room than a press conference—he tended to ramble, and his advisors had to remind him to break his points down into more media-friendly sound bites. Even his bearing was off-putting. He rarely smiled and seemed standoffish in public, looking stiff and uptight when shaking hands. "If he held up a baby," said one reporter, "it might cry." Giuliani hired a media consultant to improve his image, but it was too late to save his campaign.

Losing his race for mayor was the first major setback of Giuliani's professional life. He had gone from Manhattan College to NYU to his prestigious clerkship with Judge MacMahon without a hitch, and his career path as an attorney had been a steady rise to the top.

Instead of giving up after his defeat, Giuliani decided to regroup and try again in the next election. He studied his mistakes and committed to learning all he could about city government. He was the first to admit that while he knew a lot about law enforcement, he needed help understanding issues such as taxes, welfare, and homelessness. Because no "mayor school" existed, Giuliani created one. He started out casually interviewing authors, professors, and government officials. Then he hired Richard Schwartz, the man who would later become his senior advisor, and the project became more formal. They ended up organizing more than fifty lectures addressing how to improve the city. Giuliani brought in experts from both the Democratic and Republican parties and asked them, "If I were the mayor, what would you tell me to do?" Some of the experts would end up joining his administration when he became mayor. The lectures lasted from one to three hours and were followed by a question and answer session. "It was almost like being back at NYU," Giuliani says.

Giuliani's staff continued to try to improve his image. To prepare for negative attacks he could face from his opponent, aides prepared a top-secret "vulnerability report." The lengthy report, which was leaked to the press in 2007, analyzed Giuliani's weaknesses as a politician. It was five inches thick.

The memo warned Giuliani that his first marriage to his second cousin had created a "weirdness factor." It also recommended that Giuliani develop a softer side, saying that he had a habit of treating interviewers rudely. The report pointed out that Giuliani didn't fit neatly into either political party. His time in President Reagan's Republican administration could hurt him in liberal New York, and his support for abortion, gun control, and gay rights offended conservative voters.

The issues raised in the report would be ongoing concerns, but they weren't enough to destroy his second campaign in 1993. On November 2, Giuliani was elected the 107th mayor of New York City.

Giuliani celebrates after being elected mayor of New York. *(Courtesy of AP Images/Mark Lennihan)*

At his inauguration, all eyes were on Giuliani's seven-year-old son Andrew, who revealed a fondness for the spotlight that he obviously inherited from his dad. Uninvited, Andrew joined his father at the podium, and then hammed it up for the cameras. He imitated the mayor's hand gestures, waved to the audience and occasionally yawned. Donna called out for him to stop but he ignored her. When Giuliani appeared on the *Late Show with David Letterman*, Letterman joked that he would rather have Andrew as a guest.

During the day's ceremonies, Giuliani and Donna were inseparable. They touched affectionately and held hands. Giuliani announced two New Year's resolutions: to be the best mayor he could be, and to be the best father and husband he could be. At the party Giuliani and Donna cut a giant cake decorated with the city seal and then celebrated with 5,000 guests.

Not all New Yorkers were rejoicing in Giuliani's victory. The race had been close, and exit polls showed that New Yorkers were divided along racial lines; 85 percent of people who voted for Giuliani were white. His opponent, David Dinkins—an incumbent and New York City's first African American mayor—received most of the black vote.

Giuliani promised to make an effort to bridge the divide, but many New Yorkers felt he didn't try hard enough. The day after the election, operating on only one hour's sleep, Giuliani decided to visit all five of New York's boroughs. His first stop was Harlem, the center of black culture in the city. At the time, Harlem had high rates of crime and poverty. Giuliani promised the people of New York that "Nobody, no ethnic, religious, or racial group, will escape my care, my concern, and my attention." It was a nice promise, but not everyone was reassured.

A week after winning the election, the Giuliani family—
Giuliani, Donna, Andrew, and three-year-old Caroline—took
a four-day trip to Puerto Rico. It wasn't your typical family vacation. Giuliani spent hours each day working, holding daily press briefings and calling New York constantly.
Four of Giuliani's aides were staying at the resort, including
Giuliani's young press secretary Cristyne Lategano.

It would be the Giulianis' last vacation together as a family. Donna took the kids to Disneyworld in 1996, but dad
stayed at home. In 1998 the family went to Ireland without
him, and in 1999 they went to Paris. Giuliani told the press
he was too busy to travel.

Giuliani had a demanding schedule. He poured his heart
into cleaning up New York's streets. He started small, deal-
ing with issues that hurt the city's image and made people
feel less safe. He got rid of squeegee men by ticketing them
for jaywalking. Small successes like this boosted morale
and set the stage for larger reforms. He was following the
"Broken Windows" theory of crime: a problem that seems
minor, like a broken window in an abandoned building, can
lead to more serious problems if it's not fixed immediately.
Someone who usually wouldn't throw a rock at a window
might be more likely to if the building already has one broken window. Then all the broken windows give the area the
appearance of lawlessness, resulting in more crime.

Another of Giuliani's small victories involved taxes. The
city's high 21.25 percent hotel tax hurt tourism, one of New
York's main industries. It also discouraged business people
from visiting the city. One professional convention management association had actually boycotted the city. Giuliani
lowered the tax, and instead of seeing a loss in revenue, the

city saw an increase because more people began coming to New York.

Giuliani also launched a welfare reform program called "workfare" that partnered with a for-profit company called America Works to find jobs for welfare recipients. Inspired by President Franklin D. Roosevelt's Public Works Administration, Giuliani gave welfare recipients temporary jobs cleaning parks and answering phones.

Experts questioned the wisdom of the program, arguing that education is the best way out of dependency. Because the city didn't track participants' progress after they left their workfare job, it's not clear if the program helped prepare people for permanent employment. But workfare did succeed in reducing the number of New Yorkers on the city's welfare rolls—300,000 fewer people received welfare during Giuliani's first term. The same number left the welfare rolls during his second term.

Organized crime was another priority in the Giuliani administration. He declared war on the mafia, going after one of their biggest strongholds in the city: the Fulton Fish Market. Located in Lower Manhattan, the market had been supplying the city with seafood for 175 years. The mafia made everyone in the market pay a "protection" fee. Paying extortion to the mob meant customers ended up paying more for fish. Truckers had to pay off the mob to get their rigs loaded, and store and restaurant owners paid to have their vans "protected" while they shopped in the market. One restaurant owner who didn't understand the situation was beaten and his car destroyed because he parked in the wrong spot. Giuliani cracked down, sending in police officers and having twenty-three people arrested. The cost of fish dropped 13 percent.

The Fulton Fish Market

One of Giuliani's most notable accomplishments during his first term was the implementation of Compstat, a revolutionary tool for collecting and analyzing crime statistics. Police started studying Compstat reports on a daily basis in order to identify patterns and to try to stop problems before they spread. The *New York Times* called Compstat "probably the most powerful control device ever devised for police." Harvard University gave the program its prestigious "Innovations in Government Award" in 1996. The effect was immediate. From 1993 to 1994, major felonies fell 12.5 percent. Murder rates dropped 17.9 percent and robberies 15.5 percent. Crime was falling across the country, but New York's downturn beat the national average. Overall crime in New York City dropped 57 percent. The F.B.I. named New York the safest large city in America five years in a row.

Giuliani's popularity soared because of the drop in crime, but he wasn't without critics. His policing initiatives helped reduce crime in minority neighborhoods, but some of his other decisions offended the African American community. He refused to meet with two prominent people who disagreed with his policies: State Comptroller Carol McCall, the highest ranking African American official in state government, and Manhattan Borough President Virginia Fields, the highest ranking African American official in city government.

Slights like these prompted many people to question his commitment to healing race relations in the city. Others gave his behavior less sinister motives, attributing it to his arrogant and stubborn personality. Ed Koch, former Democratic mayor of New York and author of the book *Giuliani: Nasty Man*, says of Giuliani, "He's not a racist; he's nasty to *everybody*."

There weren't many people in New York that Giuliani did not infuriate at some point. He even managed to anger his greatest supporters, the city's Republican voters, when he endorsed Democrat Mario Cuomo in the 1994 New York governor's race. Cuomo's opponent, Republican George Pataki, went on to win the election. Giuliani would not have a friend in the new governor. The two would butt heads throughout the mayor's years in office, fighting over state budget cuts that hurt the city's drug treatment services and homeless shelters. The mayor and governor would only reconcile on 9/11, when they put their disagreements aside and joined forces in the recovery effort.

Giuliani's unpredictable behavior wasn't limited to state affairs. In 1995 it had international repercussions. At a city-sponsored event celebrating the United Nation's 50th anniversary, the mayor threw out Yasser Arafat, chairman

Giuliani would disagree with New York governor George Pataki
throughout most of his mayoral career. *(Courtesy of AP Images/Marty
Lederhandler)*

of the Palestinian Liberation Organization (PLO). Giuliani
said his aversion to Arafat went back to his days in the U.S.
Attorney's Office. As a federal prosecutor he had investigated
acts of terrorism linked to the PLO.

So when Giuliani spotted Arafat's trademark black and
white headdress in the audience at the New York Philharmonic
concert at Lincoln Center, he decided to make his feelings
known and had one of his aides tell Arafat to leave. If Giuliani

Yasser Arafat *(Courtesy of AP Images/Nasser Nasser)*

hoped his decision would win him votes in the New York
Jewish community, he was mistaken. Earlier in the day Arafat
was the invited guest at a meeting of prominent Jewish New
Yorkers. Both the United States and Israeli governments had
embraced him as a peacemaker. In fact, Arafat had recently

received the Nobel Peace Prize, together with Israel's Prime Minister Yitzhak Rabin and statesman Shimon Peres, for negotiating a peace agreement. Giuliani's brazen decision embarrassed New Yorkers and President Clinton.

Even people who looked past Giuliani's volatile personality and appreciated his skills at running the city questioned his decision to spend millions on the city's Office of Emergency

Giuliani is sworn in beside his wife, children, and mother after winning his 1997 reelection campaign. *(Courtesy of AP Images/Chang W. Lee)*

Management. He insisted that the office would prepare the city for crisis situations, including terrorist attacks. Drills and simulations would help streamline New York's response to possible plane crashes, chemical attacks, and other disasters. Giuliani had learned while working in law enforcement that surprises are going to happen, and you have to plan for the unexpected. Some people thought the O.E.M. was a waste of time and revenue. "Before September 11, there were those who said we were being overly concerned," Giuliani says.

Despite these controversies during Giuliani's first term, his changes were for the most part very popular. When he ran for reelection in 1997 against Democrat Ruth Messinger, he easily won.

But Giuliani's high approval ratings wouldn't last forever. At his second inauguration ceremony, it looked like his marriage to Donna wouldn't last either. The kissing and cuddling of the 1993 victory party was gone. Rumor had it that Giuliani was having an affair with Lategano, his top aide. At the inauguration, Donna appeared distant and withdrawn. When reporters asked her who she voted for, she refused to answer.

four
Blame and Brutality

A s Giuliani's second term progressed, the people of New York appeared to be wearying of him. The city may have become a better place to live on his watch, but his critics—who were increasing in number—doubted Giuliani alone was responsible for the improvement.

New York magazine ran an ad on the side of buses calling itself "possibly the only good thing in New York Giuliani hasn't taken credit for." Giuliani was enraged at the ads and forced the Transit Authority to take them down. The magazine sued and won. He appealed, trying to take the case all the way to the Supreme Court. They refused to hear it, but the damage was already done—New Yorkers saw the episode as evidence of Giuliani's out-of-control ego.

Three major cases of police brutality threatened to destroy his legacy. In August 1997, officers arrested Haitian immigrant Abner Louima outside a Brooklyn nightclub. Louima, a married father of two, was one of several men who intervened

In 1997, Abner Louima was beaten, tortured, and raped by New York policemen. *(Courtesy of AP Images/Ed Betz)*

in a fight between two women at the club. Police called to the scene arrested him, and, on the ride to the station, they beat him with their fists, batons, and handheld radios. At the precinct, they strip-searched him and put him in a holding cell. Later that night, a patrol officer tortured and raped Louima with a broomstick in a bathroom. Louima had to be hospitalized for two months after the assault.

Less than two years after the Louima tragedy, in February 1999, Amadou Diallo, a twenty-three-year-old immigrant from Guinea, was standing on top of his apartment building looking down on the street below. Four plainclothes police officers passing by thought his behavior looked suspicious and decided to question him. When Diallo reached inside his coat the officers fired forty-one shots. As Diallo lay dying in the doorway, one of the officers checked his hand and saw that the object he had been reaching for was his wallet.

One year later there was yet another shooting. Patrick Dorismond, an off duty and unarmed Haitian security guard, was standing on the street when undercover officers approached him and asked him to sell them drugs. Dorismond told them he wasn't a drug dealer. Then, for some reason, he and the undercover police officers got into a fight. During the scuffle one of the officers shot Dorismond in the heart.

After each case Giuliani came to the police officer's defense. To many New Yorkers, the mayor seemed willing to forgive the police for any infraction. After Dorismond was shot, for example, the mayor broke state law and released Dorismond's juvenile delinquency record. Even Giuliani's most loyal supporters were shocked when the mayor told the media that Dorismond wasn't exactly "an altar boy."

The fact all three victims were African American did not surprise everyone, even some of Giuliani's supporters. Lilliam Barrios-Paoli, a former member of the Giuliani administration, says that the culture of the NYPD was a factor in the shootings. She attributed a good deal of that dysfunctional culture to the fact that too many police officers did not live in the city. "There's a new category of liability: 'WWB, walking while black,'" she said. "They see a big black guy

Throughout the allegations of police brutality, Giuliani always came to the defense of the NYPD. *(Courtesy of AP Images/Todd Plitt)*

and they're scared. And guess what? They assume things. If you've lived in New York, you *don't* automatically assume that if you see black kids coming toward you, they're going to mug you. But when you have a police force that works in the city but doesn't live in the city, it's a problem."

Giuliani was criticized for tolerating an anti-black bias in his police department and for allowing officers to engage in racial profiling. He was charged with encouraging the police to go to any measure to lower crime. Although police shootings actually declined 40 percent during Giuliani's administration, this fact was overshadowed by the brutality of these three highly publicized cases—and by Giuliani's reaction to them.

If Giuliani failed to react strongly enough to wrongdoing in his police department, some people in the city felt he reacted too strongly to other problems. New Yorkers prided themselves on their city's gutsy, gritty reputation. Giuliani's fines for rude cab drivers and owners of noisy car alarms seemed at odds with the spirit of the city. His policies may have made New York more appealing to tourists, but some New Yorkers felt it eroded the city's uniqueness.

Giuliani's reaction to an art exhibition caused even more controversy. In the fall of 1999, the Brooklyn Museum of Art ran an exhibit called "Sensation." Giuliani didn't see

Giuliani was offended by one of the exhibits in the Sensation art show, and pledged to cut off city funding for the Brooklyn Museum of Art unless the piece was removed. *(Courtesy of AP Images/Diane Bondareff)*

the art in person, but when he looked through the exhibition catalog he was shocked at one painting in particular. "The Holy Virgin Mary," by African American Catholic artist Chris Ofili pictured a black Virgin Mary adorned with elephant dung. Pinned around her were small photographs of nude women.

Giuliani called the exhibit "sick stuff," stopped the city's funding, and tried to get the museum evicted from Brooklyn. The museum took the case to court and won. Ofili, they pointed out, often used elephant dung as a positive reference to his African heritage. The nude photos were contemporary versions of little naked cherubs—figures often used in traditional religious art by such artists as Donatello and Raphael. The court ruled that Giuliani's actions amounted to censorship.

The next year, Giuliani's policies came under even greater scrutiny. New York's Democratic Senator Daniel Moynihan had announced his retirement, and Giuliani began gearing up for the 2000 election, hoping to fill the soon-to-be vacant seat. Early in the race the Republican Party feared Governor Pataki and his allies would try to sabotage Giuliani's campaign. The Governor initially supported another candidate, Republican Congressman Rick Lazio. The state's position angered Republicans in Washington, who saw Giuliani as their best shot at capturing the Senate seat. After months of fundraising, Giuliani made more than $9 million and was considered a shoo-in to capture the Republican Party's nomination.

His Democratic opponent was Hillary Clinton, President Bill Clinton's wife and the outgoing First Lady of the United States. It was the first time a first lady had run for public

Hillary Clinton

office. She and Giuliani were both stars of their parties and the race drew the whole country's attention.

Controversy over Clinton's residency also made headlines. A year before the race, the Clintons, not New York natives, bought a house in Chappaqua, a town north of New York City. She was accused of being a "carpetbagger," a derogatory term coined after the Civil War to describe Northerners who moved to the South for profit or in order to obtain political office. (The Northerners carried their belongings in inexpensive pieces of luggage called carpetbags.) The term carpetbagger expanded to include any outsider suspected of exploiting an area for political gain, but it lost much of its sting in the 20th century, especially in New York. In 1964, Robert Kennedy moved to New York from Virginia amid the same accusations. Voters didn't mind and elected him senator. Clinton was determined that her campaign would also overcome the carpetbagger issue. She carried out a statewide "listening tour," meeting residents and local government officials in each of New York's sixty-two counties.

Clinton's decision to run came on the heels of a scandal that troubled her husband's last two years in office. In January 1998 the story broke that President Clinton had had an affair with 22-year-old White House intern Monica Lewinsky. It wasn't the first time Bill Clinton was suspected of having an illicit extramarital relationship. Paula Jones, an Arkansas state employee, had recently sued Clinton for sexual harassment. She said that he exposed himself to her during a professional meeting in his hotel room years earlier when he was governor. Jones's lawyers questioned the President and several women who they believed had been involved with him, including Monica

Bill Clinton

Lewinsky. Clinton testified under oath that he had not had sexual relations with Lewinsky. He later changed his story, confessing to the affair with Lewinsky and opening himself up to charges of perjury and obstruction of justice. In December the House Judiciary Committee voted along party lines to impeach Clinton. Congressman Lazio voted for the impeachment; Giuliani strongly opposed it. President Clinton was acquitted of all charges after a twenty-one day trial. He settled the Jones lawsuit by paying her almost $1 million. A judge in the case ordered Clinton to pay a fine for giving false testimony, and suspended his license to practice law.

Throughout the scandal Hillary Clinton supported her husband, winning sympathy for her dignified response. Bill Clinton's legacy was tarnished by the controversy, but the First Lady's reputation was only enhanced.

Hillary Clinton's commitment to her marriage was a dramatic contrast to Giuliani's rumored history of infidelity. In the months leading up to the state Republican Party's May 30 nomination convention, the media started picking up on problems in his marriage with Donna Hanover. He had started appearing in public with his girlfriend Judith Nathan, a former nurse and pharmaceutical sales representative. For months Giuliani and Nathan had been spending long weekends at her beach condo in Southampton, New York. In the city the two of them became regulars at Cuker's, a cigar bar near her home. They shared a private, curtained-off room. Giuliani told reporters that Nathan was "a very good friend,"

Giuliani's infidelity left him open to charges of hypocrisy. On an episode of *Saturday Night Live*, comedian Tina Fey joked, "Giuliani is once again expressing his outrage at an art exhibit. . . . Said the mayor: 'This trash is not the sort of thing that I want to look at when I go to the museum with my mistress.'"

In May 2000 Giuliani told reporters he was separating from his wife Donna Hanover (she had kept her maiden name). However, he had failed to tell his wife about his decision first. Donna Hanover came back with her own statement to the press. "For several years it was difficult to participate in Rudy's public life because of his relationship with one staff member," she told reporters. Donna's spokesperson later confirmed she was referring to Giuliani's alleged affair with his aide Cristyne Lategano.

Giuliani and Hanover were soon at war, and their bickering and divorce proceedings filled the papers. Hanover and the couple's two children stayed in Gracie Mansion, the official residence for the mayor of New York, but Giuliani moved out.

The same week Giuliani announced his separation, the public found out he was facing another personal crisis. He had recently been diagnosed with prostate cancer, the same disease that had killed his father nineteen years earlier. Complicating matters was Giuliani's 2000 Senate campaign. As Giuliani tried to decide on a course of treatment, he found himself thinking too much about the upcoming election. He knew he couldn't give both the race and his health his full attention.

In an emotional press conference less than a month after his diagnosis, Giuliani announced he was dropping out of the senate race. "Because I've been in public life so long and politics," he said, "I used to think the core of me was in politics probably. It isn't." His voice was uncharacteristically nervous, and he went on to reveal a side of himself New Yorkers hadn't seen before. When facing illness, he said, "something beautiful happens. It makes you figure out what you're really all about and what's really important to you."

He went on to say that he considered himself lucky. "The reason I'm such a fortunate man is that I have people that love me, and I love them, and they care for me and I care for them. And that's the greatest support that you can have in life."

This kinder, gentler Giuliani then promised to reach out to minorities and devote his last eighteen months in office to becoming a better mayor. At the end of Giuliani's speech, a reporter asked him if he felt closer to God. "I hope he's closer to me," he answered.

five
September 11

I n September 2001, Giuliani had successfully completed cancer treatment and was looking ahead to his last four months in office.

The morning of September 11 dawned bright and clear—a beautiful day in New York City. The skyline was beautiful against a brilliant, cloudless blue.

As Giuliani finished up a breakfast meeting at the Peninsula Hotel, an aide's phone rang a few minutes before nine o'clock. It was the deputy mayor calling to tell Giuliani that a plane had crashed into the World Trade Center. It might be a small private plane, he said, but no one was sure if it was deliberate or an accident. Giuliani looked up at the clear sky and knew instantly that the collision hadn't been an accident.

It was Giuliani's policy to go and to see with his own eyes the scene of any crisis. When he was a young attorney, a detective taught him to get as much information as possible firsthand. For example, if a witness claimed they heard

When the second plane crashed into the World Trade Center, Giuliani knew the city was being attacked by terrorists.
(Courtesy of AP Images/Carmen Taylor)

the front door slam, detectives and lawyers needed to know if the building had a revolving door.

That morning Giuliani did what he always did and went straight to the scene. He was concerned but not overly anxious. The city was prepared for a wide variety of crisis situations. The Office of Emergency Management had been running drills and simulations to prepare for terrorist attacks. But no one could have prepared for what was about to unfold.

Giuliani and his aides sped toward the Emergency Command Center at Seven World Trade Center, not knowing it would be unusable. On their way there they passed St. Vincent's, one of the hospitals closest to the World Trade Center. Doctors and nurses were standing outside in their operating gowns, waiting with stretchers to receive the wounded. It was an alarming sight. "It had to be even worse than I thought," Giuliani remembers thinking.

A second plane hit the other tower at 9:03, minutes before Giuliani arrived on the scene. He saw the flash of fire, but he assumed it was secondary explosion in the first tower. Patti Varrone, a member of the mayor's security detail, got the call from Police Command informing them that the South Tower had been hit. Giuliani now knew without a doubt it was terrorism.

He and his aides continued trying to call the White House, but heavy cell phone traffic in the area crashed the network. Using cell phones would become next to impossible after the North Tower collapsed because three major transmitters were located on top of the building.

In the coming hours and days, details about the attacks would begin to emerge. Nineteen hijackers affiliated with the terrorist organization al-Qaeda carried out the attacks. The first plane to hit was American Airlines Flight 11 from Boston. It crashed into the North Tower at 8:45 a.m. With minutes, at 9:03, the second hijacked airliner, United Airlines Flight 175, also from Boston, crashed into the South Tower. At 9:43 American Airlines Flight 77 from Washington, D.C., crashed into the Pentagon. At 10:10 a.m. United Airlines Flight 93 from Newark, New Jersey crashed in Somerset County, Pennsylvania, southeast of Pittsburgh. Government officials suspect its intended target was either the White House or U.S. Capitol Building.

When Giuliani and his aides arrived at the command center, they found that the building was being evacuated because it was too close to the Twin Towers. Now Giuliani and his team didn't have a secure headquarters from which to coordinate emergency services. He needed to establish a new command center quickly and find a way to communicate with people of New York.

With the Emergency Command Center unavailable, city officials decided to set up two command posts—one for the Fire Department and one for the Police Department. The Fire Department would be leading the rescue and evacuation, and the Police Department had to protect the rest of the city and communicate with the state and federal government.

As Giuliani's group turned onto West Street, the mayor got his first full view of the towers. The tops of the buildings were in flames. To avoid being hit by falling debris, Giuliani and the others looked up as they walked. He saw falling rubble, and then something else caught his eye—about a hundred stories up the North Tower, a man jumped from a window. Then two people jumped together, holding hands as they fell. Giuliani realized they were making a conscious decision to end their lives rather than endure the inferno inside. He grabbed the Police Commissioner's arm and said, "We're in unchartered waters now."

Giuliani stopped by the Fire Department's temporary command post before going on to his final destination at 75 Barclay Street. Thinking of the people he saw jumping from the tower, Giuliani asked Fire Chief Peter Ganci if it would be possible to use helicopters to save the people on the floors above the fire. Ganci told him that the smoke wouldn't let helicopters get close enough to lift people to safety. Firefighters were already on their way up the towers, and Ganci expected that they could save everyone below the fire. Giuliani understood what Ganci was saying: except for the lucky few who might find a safe stairwell, everyone above the point of impact was lost.

Giuliani shook Ganci's hand and said "God bless you." He said goodbye to First Deputy Commissioner Bill Feehan and waved to Battalion Chief Ray Downey and wished them all luck. Father Mychal Judge, the Fire Department's chaplain, rushed by and Giuliani reached for his hand. The mayor had known these men for years, pinned medals on them and looked up to them as heroes. All four died that day.

Giuliani left and made his way to 75 Barclay Street, where he and his staff took over a group of empty cubicles on the ground floor and used the landlines to call the White

Fire Chief Peter Ganci died while trying to rescue people following the terrorist attacks. *(Courtesy of AP Images/Chitose Suzuki)*

When the first tower collapsed, Giuliani and his staff were trapped in their temporary command center. *(Courtesy of AP Images/Jim Collins)*

House. As soon as Giuliani got Deputy Assistant to the President Chris Henick on the phone, he asked him if New York had air cover in case more attacks were planned. Henick told him that they had dispatched jets twelve minutes earlier and that they would arrive any minute. Giuliani then asked if it was true that a plane had crashed into the Pentagon. Henick confirmed that the Pentagon had been attacked.

First the World Trade Center, then the Pentagon—Giuliani had to prepare for the possibility of more attacks. He tried to get into the terrorists' heads and imagine what they would target next— the Statue of Liberty, the Empire State Building, the United Nations, the Stock Exchange? Would the terrorists detonate bombs, take hostages, or use biological weapons? As these thoughts ran through his head, Giuliani had to deal with the existing emergency at the World Trade Center.

As a precautionary measure the White House was being evacuated. Henick told Giuliani that Vice President Dick Cheney would call as soon he could. In a few minutes the vice president did call back, but before he and Giuliani had a chance to talk, the phone went dead. Seconds later Police Department Chief Joe Esposito yelled, "It's coming down— everybody down!"

The ground quaked and there was a loud roar. Barclay's south-facing windows shattered and the room filled with black smoke. Giuliani, still in a cubicle trying to call the Vice President, had no idea what had happened. Even with debris falling all around him, it was unimaginable that one of the Twin Towers could have collapsed. Maybe, he thought, it was the radio tower on top of the World Trade Center that had fallen. The World Trade Center, after all, had survived a bombing in 1993 that blew a hundred foot hole through four floors. The two towers seemed like giant fortresses. The architects had designed them to withstand high winds as well as accidental collisions from small planes.

Giuliani decided to get everyone out of 75 Barclay, but piles of concrete, broken glass, and tangled steel cables blocked the exits. They went downstairs to try the doors in the basement and discovered that all of them were locked. Then suddenly two maintenance men appeared and guided the mayor and his staff through a maze of tunnels that led them into the lobby of the adjoining building. The mayor's relief turned to horror when he saw the horror outside. Dark clouds of dust eclipsed the sun that had shined so brightly moments before. The air was thick with smoke. Seeing objects flying through the air, Giuliani thought to himself that it looked like the tornado scene in *The Wizard of Oz*.

As the mayor and his team took in the sight before them, a man walked into the lobby coated with soot. His eyes were bleeding. It was Tibor Kerekes, a close friend of the mayor. A courageous martial artist with a black belt in karate, Kerekes was shaking. "It's terrible out there," he said. "Terrible."

When Kerekes told them that the South Tower had collapsed, Giuliani had to decide what to do. The police officers in the group recommended that everyone stay put until they had more information, but the mayor didn't want to

As the second tower collapsed, Giuliani was forced to run from the dust and debris generated by the falling building. *(Courtesy of AP Images/ Amy Sancetta)*

lose a second. He knew the people of New York needed to hear from him. And he had another feeling that he kept to himself. "If I have to die," he thought, "I'd rather die outside than get trapped in a building."

Once outside, Giuliani ran into a group of journalists. He held a walking press conference, telling the reporters that people needed to stay calm and walk north, away from the attack site. Everyone they passed on the street he tried to herd northward. "We are kind of like pied pipers, you know, shooing everybody north. He is the perfect guy for it," says Fire Commissioner Tom Von Essen. "I remember him grabbing a few people, saying, 'Careful, take it easy, just keep walking!'"

As the group walked north, the second building collapsed. Giuliani and his team ran for their lives, chased by a surge of dust and debris from the tower. Moments later they heard a plane overhead, and everyone was relieved to see it was a U.S. Navy jet. Giuliani had a passing thought—how strange that New York City had become a battlefield.

The mayor had to force his mind to focus on the task at hand—the city government needed a place to work. The first location they tried, the Tribeca Grand Hotel, wouldn't do. Giuliani marched right back out as soon as he saw the hotel's windowed atrium. He had seen enough raining glass that morning.

The group decided to try a nearby firehouse. When they arrived it was closed—all the firefighters had left to join the rescue effort at the Twin Towers. Finally someone was able to pick the lock. Once inside, Giuliani held his first real press conference.

His goal was to calm people down and help them evacuate safely. At the time, he still didn't know if additional attacks would follow. After the mayor's press conference, he and his aides arranged for extra security at potential targets. Only after that was taken care of did Giuliani turn his full attention to his family and loved ones. He had heard they were safe, but he hadn't had a chance to speak with them. He called Donna and they agreed she and the children would go to New Jersey for the night. After that he called Judith Nathan. He told her it would be safest if she stayed in her apartment, but she was anxious to see him in person. She drove south toward the danger zone to meet him.

After visiting Ground Zero after the collapse of the towers, Giuliani began to realize there would not be many survivors amid the ruins. *(Courtesy of AP Images/Graham Morrison)*

By this time city officials had found a new home base for Giuliani's team at the Police Academy on 20th Street. When Giuliani arrived, Judith Nathan was already there comforting members of his administration. His longtime executive assistant, Beth Petrone, had lost her husband, firefighter Terence Hatton, in the towers when they collapsed. His death was unconfirmed, but Petrone knew without being told that he had died. Other members of the city government had been at the World Trade Center that morning, and no one knew how many had survived.

Nathan, with years of experience in the health care industry, knew the local hospitals well. Giuliani put her to work making sure there were enough beds available to care for the injured.

Late that afternoon, Giuliani met with Dr. Charles S. Hirsch, New York City's medical examiner. Dr. Hirsch said it was unlikely that many people would be recovered alive from the ruins. Giuliani, a self-described optimist, didn't want to believe him. He ordered rescue teams to work around the clock, and his staff scrambled to run electricity to the site so that the area could be illuminated overnight.

During one of his five visits to Ground Zero that day, Giuliani began to acknowledge that surviving the wreckage was unlikely. Where New York's tallest buildings had stood hours earlier was now sixteen acres of smoldering wreckage. Scattered fires created a hellish glow.

Dr. Hirsch's terrible prediction turned out to be right. Giuliani and Nathan stayed in touch with the city's hospitals, making sure beds, doctors, and donated blood would be available for the thousands of injured they expected to check in. It didn't happen. No one was recovered alive in the days after the attack.

Throughout the day, Giuliani faced constant pressure from the media to estimate the number of causalities. Some members of his staff thought that they should provide a figure, otherwise it would look like the mayor didn't know enough about what was going on. "I decided right away not to play guessing games with lost lives," says Giuliani. "I told them the truth: 'When we get the final number, it will be more than we can bear.'"

It wasn't long after the planes hit the Twin Towers that it became evident that the terrorists were Arab. Giuliani immediately warned the people of New York not to react against any particular group of people. He made it clear that the city would not tolerate intimidation or violence. "Hatred, prejudice, and anger are what caused this terrible tragedy, and the people of New York should act differently," he said. "We should act bravely. We should act in a tolerant way. We should go about our business, and we should show these people that they can't stop us." To help reduce harassment against Arab Americans, Giuliani created a category in the Compstat system to monitor any incidents and put a stop to them before they became a widespread problem.

At a press conference that night, Giuliani told the people of New York and the world, "It's going to be a very difficult time. I don't think we yet know the pain we're going to feel. But the thing we have to focus on now is getting the city through this and surviving and being stronger for it. New York is still here."

That night, after telling his staff to go home and rest up for the days ahead, Giuliani returned to Ground Zero. Under flood lights, rescue workers dug through the ruins—mounds of concrete, building materials, and office equipment. Like people all over the country seeing the same scene on their televisions, he couldn't believe his eyes. Giuliani allowed himself to feel anger and grief for only a few moments, and then forced himself to refocus on the city's needs.

Late that night—or actually 2:30 the next morning—Giuliani finally made it back to the apartment he was sharing with friends. He was still coated in dust, but was too tired to shower. He turned on the television and watched the footage of the towers collapsing over and over and over again. He undressed and lay out a new set of clothes in case something happened during the night. On his nightstand was Roy Jenkins' biography of Winston Churchill, the British statesmen who led his country through the darkest days of World War II. Giuliani thought about the daily bombings the people of London endured, and how they managed to go on with their lives and ultimately prevail. He fell asleep at 4:30 a.m. and woke up less than an hour later. He waited for the sun to rise, and felt grateful when it did. "Now it was our turn to fight back," he said.

six

America's Mayor

When Giuliani became mayor, there were those who doubted his crime fighting experience was enough to keep New Yorkers safe in a true emergency. Protecting people from pickpockets was one thing, but terrorism was something else. "The question, among critics, was almost always the same," wrote a journalist for *The New York Times* in 1993. "Though he might be a competent manager, what would Giuliani do in a crisis? In a riot? At a moment of truth?"

Giuliani seized the challenge of September 11, 2001, as if it was what he was born to do. He tackled multiple roles on the fly and handled all of them. He was a calm, steady hand in the middle of chaos, giving cool-headed updates throughout the day. He got everyone working together, coordinating at the city, state, and federal level. He consoled the nation—addressing the people of American with compassion and empathy—just like he consoled families at the more than two hundred funerals he attended in the days afterward. He was a bold decision maker, reopening the New York Stock Exchange, Major League Baseball, and Broadway theaters within days of the attack in order to demonstrate the city's resiliency.

People around the world praised Giuliani for his heroic leadership, including his instinct to head toward the danger zone instead of away from it. Former first lady Nancy Reagan presented him with the Ronald Reagan Presidential Freedom Award; he was knighted by the Queen of England; French President Jacques Chirac dubbed him the Rock. *Time* magazine named him Person of the Year. Giuliani said he was just doing his job. "I was mayor. Part of my job description was to coordinate and supervise emergencies," he says.

Twenty-five thousand people were evacuated from the Twin Towers, making it the largest rescue in America's history. Fewer than one hundred people below the point of impact died, meaning 99.5 percent of the people who could be saved were saved. But the 2,843 lives lost made Ground Zero the largest mass grave on American soil in the country's history. Among the casualties were 344 members of the Fire Department and twenty-three police officers. At the Pentagon, 234 people died. Twenty percent of Americans know someone lost or injured in the 9/11 attacks.

For days after the attacks, friends and family members of the missing filled the streets of Manhattan, going from hospital to hospital searching for their loved ones. Relatives covered telephone poles, fences, and lampposts with missing-persons flyers. Photos of the missing were posted alongside identifying details, such as birthmarks and tattoos.

Friends and relatives of those missing blanketed Manhattan with
missing-persons flyers. *(AP Images/Kathy Willens)*

One of Giuliani's most pressing concerns was setting up a place for the thousands of relatives to find information and assistance. New York Governor George Pataki gave the city access to the National Guard Armory on Lexington Avenue. The huge building was a good short-term solution, but Giuliani didn't like how dark and depressing it was. To make matters worse, the building was uncomfortably hot.

The line of mothers, fathers, husbands, wives, brothers, and sisters snaked around the block. Their loved ones hadn't contacted them. Their names weren't on the list of the known dead. Against all odds the families hoped that their loved ones would be found alive. They wanted to know if there were survivors in the hospitals, alive but unidentified. Giuliani had to tell them the truth—it was a very small number. One question in particular—Are there people alive in the hospitals with amnesia?—showed the families' heartbreaking desperation.

Giuliani knew the city needed a better location for the families to gather, and he made it a priority to find one. He wanted it to be near the center of government so that city officials could spend as much time there as possible. There were already plans to move the command center from the Police Academy to Pier 92 on the Hudson River. Pier 94, immediately north, would be a huge improvement over the armory.

Volunteers quickly transformed the 125,000-square-foot space into a comfortable Family Assistance Center. There was a counseling center, DNA collection offices (for identifying family members), emergency financial services, and child care.

In the aftermath of 9/11, Giuliani's friendship with Governor George Pataki wasn't his only unlikely alliance. He began working closely with New York Senator Hillary Clinton, his brief adversary in the 2000 Senate race. Together with New York Senator Chuck Schumer, Giuliani and Clinton secured $20 billion in federal aid for New York City.

On September 23, Yankee Stadium hosted an interfaith prayer service for the relatives and friends of victims. One of Giuliani's staff members questioned the appropriateness of the location, but Giuliani pointed out that Pope John Paul II had celebrated Mass there. Even though the ballpark is one of the symbols of the city, it was not everyone's first choice. The city hoped they could hold the service in Central Park, but it was rejected because it was too risky security-wise.

The September 23 prayer service at Yankee Stadium was organized in five days and without any funding. *(Courtesy of AP Images/Richard Drew)*

Yankee Stadium ended up serving as the place for New Yorkers to come together and memorialize those who had lost their lives.

Rudy Washington, Giuliani's deputy mayor, was responsible for organizing the service, and he only had five days to do it—and no money. Giuliani wouldn't let him use a single cent of the money coming in for the victims' families. Washington was afraid he wouldn't be able to get public figures to participate on such short notice, but he was overwhelmed by the response. He approached fifteen people, including Oprah Winfrey and James Earl Jones, and all of them said yes. Placido Domingo sang "Ave Maria," one of the mayor's favorite hymns. Flight routes over the stadium were altered so that the noise of their engines would not interfere with the service.

In the days following the attacks, Giuliani didn't have much time to mourn the lifelong friends he had lost. For the most part he kept up a calm exterior hour after hour, week after week, but there were moments when he couldn't control his emotions. He'd go to four funerals one day and not shed a tear, but at the fifth he'd see a boy holding his father's FDNY helmet and the tears would well up.

The rest of the world was finally seeing a side of the mayor that only his friends were privy to, but it was not to be the dawn of Giuliani the Gentle. His notorious aggressiveness showed up on the one-month anniversary of the attacks. Saudi Prince al-Waleed bin Talal, one of the world's richest men, gave Giuliani a cashier's check for $10 million for the Twin Towers Fund. Giuliani took him on a tour of Ground Zero, just as he had taken world leaders like Nelson Mandela, Tony Blair, and Russian President Vladimir Putin.

Although Giuliani was able to remain calm in the days following the attacks, there were times when he became emotional over the loss of friends and colleagues. *(Courtesy of AP Images/Kathy Willens)*

As Giuliani and the Prince took in the ruins, Giuliani felt that something was wrong. The Prince expressed his condolences, but he seemed unmoved. Giuliani even detected a smirk on his face.

After the tour, the Prince had released a press release announcing his donation. He also used the release to criticize the U.S. government's support of Israel, suggesting that American foreign policy had led to the attack. Giuliani's first reaction was to give the money back. He hesitated, thinking of the families of the firefighters and police officers the money would help, but he finally decided to reject the donation. Relatives of victims told Giuliani they supported his decision. "A surprising number of them used the same phrase," he

Prince al-Waleed bin Talal *(Courtesy of AP Images)*

says, "'We don't want his blood money.' Not a single person ever came up to me and said I should have kept it."

The same day Giuliani met with the Saudi Prince, he sat down with a group of advertising executives. Because tourism is a crucial part of New York's economy, the city's recovery depended on visitors. Famous New Yorkers like Woody Allen, Barbara Walters, and Yogi Berra starred in the ads, and television networks ran the spots free or at a heavily reduced rate. A spirit of giving flooded the city. From people assisting with the cleanup effort at Ground Zero to those who donated blood in the hours after the attack, there were so many volunteers that the city couldn't find enough for them to do. "New York is still here," Giuliani told the world. "New York is going to be here tomorrow morning, and it's going to be here forever."

As he had on September 11th, Giuliani continued to think of Churchill in the following weeks. The Prime Minister's inspiring speeches had encouraged frightened Londoners during Nazi Germany's months of air raids. Giuliani wanted to lift his peoples' spirits the same way Churchill had.

Winston Churchhill *(Library of Congress)*

Looking back on Churchill's positive words, Giuliani wonders how much of it was a bluff. Churchill could not have known England would triumph. He only hoped.

Was Giuliani's confidence a bluff? "In a crisis you have to be optimistic," he says. "When I said the spirit of the city would be stronger, I didn't know that. I just hoped it. There are parts of you that say, Maybe we're not going to get through this. You don't listen to them."

President George Bush was in Florida reading to a group of children when the attacks occurred. He

Giuliani and Secretary of Defense Donald Rumsfeld speak at a press conference at the site of the 9/11 attacks. *(Courtesy of Department of Defense; official photo by Robert D. Ward)*

came across to many as unprepared and out of the loop, especially when contrasted with Giuliani. The mayor was the nation's acting wartime spokesperson, and Americans were grateful for his leadership. Roy Jenkins, author of the biography that inspired Giuliani the night of September 11, told *Time* magazine, "What Giuliani succeeded in doing is what Churchill succeeded in doing in the dreadful summer of 1940: he managed to create an illusion that we were bound to win."

When Giuliani announced in May of 2000 that he was bowing out of the Senate race to focus on his cancer treatment, he said he wanted to dedicate the rest of mayoralty to breaking down barriers. In the end, it was Giuliani's performance on that tragic day and the days afterward that unified his city. The same way Churchill had offered his countrymen his "blood, toil, tears, and sweat" sixty years before, Giuliani gave freely of himself to the people of New York on September 11 and in the days afterward. He hadn't always been able to show it, but on 9/11 Giuliani proved to New Yorkers just how much he cared.

seven
20/20 Hindsight

I n the months following the September 11, 2001, attacks, the American people demanded answers. Could the terrorist strikes have been prevented? Who decided that New York's emergency offices would be located in the World Trade Center? Why didn't the Police and Fire Departments communicate better during the rescue effort?

With the aid of hindsight, some New Yorkers criticized Giuliani for his decision to locate the city's Emergency Command Center on the 23rd floor the World Trade Center. Because the site had been bombed in 1993, people thought he should have known better than to build such an important and expensive office at a known target.

Giuliani received the most criticism for the communication breakdown that occurred during the rescue effort. The Fire Department had problems with their radios, which resulted in many of the firefighters inside the World Trade Center working without any information from the outside. The most catastrophic decision was the Fire Department's failure to evacuate the South Tower when the North Tower was hit; and when the South Tower collapsed, the Fire Department didn't evacuate their people from the North Tower. The firefighters continued working, unaware that the other tower had fallen.

To make things worse, the police and fire departments didn't share information that could have saved lives. They failed to coordinate their search for civilians inside the World Trade Center, losing precious time when the same floors were covered by both agencies. The Police Department helicopters had important information that could have helped the firefighters below, but they weren't able to share it with the FDNY in time.

Would the two departments have communicated better if they had shared a single command center? With the city's Emergency Command Center in the WTC unusable, and no backup office available, Giuliani says the separate sites were the best option because of the agencies' different needs. The Police Department had to work at 75 Barclay because they needed telephone lines to communicate with the Defense Department, governor, and White House. The Fire Department needed a location within sight of the fire.

After months of investigations, a bipartisan panel determined that the city's response on 9/11 was imperfect but commendable. In *The 9/11 Commission Report*, they wrote, "The emergency response to the attacks on 9/11 was necessarily improvised. In New York, the FDNY, NYPD, the Port Authority, WTC employees, and the building occupants themselves did their best to cope with the effects of an unimaginable catastrophe—unfolding furiously over a mere 102 minutes—

for which they were unprepared in terms of both training and mindset. As a result of the efforts of first responders, assistance from each other, and their own good instincts and goodwill, the vast majority of civilians below the impact zone were able to evacuate the towers."

In mid-September, while the country was still reeling from the devastation of 9/11, some offices in New York City discovered anthrax spores in their mail. Erin O'Connor, Tom

THE

9/11

COMMISSION
REPORT

FINAL REPORT OF THE NATIONAL COMMISSION ON TERRORIST ATTACKS UPON THE UNITED STATES

Despite allegations to the contrary, the 9/11 Commission found that Giuliani's response to the terrorist attacks was appropriate and commendable.

Brokaw's assistant at NBC Nightly News, opened two envelopes—one contained a sandlike substance and the other a white powder. Days later she developed a lesion on her chest. Her doctor sent a biopsy sample to the Centers for Disease Control and Prevention, and it tested positive for anthrax. No one immediately made the connection between the pieces of mail and the infection. When other cases began popping up in October, authorities at first assumed they were isolated

Letter to Tom Brokaw

Letter to Senator Daschle

These two envelopes, sent to Tom Brokaw and Senator Tom Daschle, contained potentially lethal anthrax spores. *(Courtesy of AP Images/Justice Department)*

cases picked up from natural sources (wild animals sometimes carry anthrax). But soon it became clear that someone was sending the deadly spores through the mail. Suspicious letters showed up in the offices of other prominent figures in the media and politics, including NBC's Tom Brokaw, South Dakota Senator Tom Daschle, and New York Governor George Pataki.

In Washington, D.C., the U.S. Capitol shut down, and there were anthrax threats and hoaxes all over the country. People were afraid to open their mail. Early reports called the bacteria a biological weapon, and many Americans feared that anthrax was a new terrorist threat that put everyone in the country at risk, not just New Yorkers. Giuliani wanted people to stay calm. He decided right away that investigators in hazmat suits in the city's office buildings would not be shown on television. He didn't want to exaggerate the threat and give the people another reason to panic.

On November 3rd Giuliani was in Arizona with his son and daughter for Game Six of the World Series, cheering on the Yankees. During the eighth inning he received a call from New York Health Commissioner Neal Cohen telling him that anthrax had been found in City Hall, about twenty feet from his office. He flew back to New York that night. "The last thing the city needed to see was an image of City Hall shutting its doors," he says. Most people at risk for exposure took Cipro, the antibiotic effective in treating the infection, but Giuliani refused. He thought the real danger was panic, not the anthrax bacteria.

The anthrax mailings—and the hoaxes—soon stopped, but not before five people died. No one was charged with the crime; it's possible an individual was responsible and not a terrorist organization.

Giuliani was a stabilizing influence in the shaky months following the World Trade Center attacks, and New Yorkers were reluctant to elect a new mayor during their recovery efforts. Term limit laws prevented him from running for a third term, but everywhere the mayor went he was met with cries of "Four more years, four more years." The primary day, which had been scheduled for September 11,[th] was postponed until the 25th, but even by then many weren't ready to elect a new mayor. There was talk of changing the law to allow Giuliani a third term, or extending his term by two or three months to ease the transition. In the end, the state ruled that an extension was not necessary.

Giuliani backed Republican candidate Michael Bloomberg, a political novice and media tycoon worth billions. Bloomberg was a lifelong Democrat who changed his party affiliation the year before the election. He spent an estimated $41 million of his own money on his campaign. With Giuliani's endorsement, the city of New York elected him mayor. He won by only 4,200 votes, but that was all he needed.

With the help of Giuliani's endorsement, Michael Bloomberg *(left)* became mayor of New York. *(Courtesy of AP Images/Robert Spencer)*

December 31, 2001, was Giuliani's last day as mayor. As he had everyday for eight years, he started business with a morning meeting. They discussed a last-minute deal they were trying to get signed with the New York Stock Exchange and went over year-end crime figures. Giuliani thanked his staff for their excellent work, and then he went downstairs to his empty office. Almost everything was packed, including his hundreds of baseball caps and other keepsakes. Only a few personal items were left: a couple of photographs, a brief case from the early '70s when he was an assistant U.S. attorney, and a medal he had received from the Fire Department for going into a burning church in 1992 and evacuating parishioners and the priest.

That night was New Year's Eve, and Giuliani's last act as mayor was to ring in 2002. Standing in Times Square with more than half a million revelers, at the stroke of midnight he pressed the button to drop the ball in Times Square. A few minutes later he gave the oath of office to his successor.

eight
Life After City Hall

On New Year's Day 2002, Rudy Giuliani was a private citizen for the first time in eight years. Before leaving for Florida on a short vacation, he attended Mike Bloomberg's inauguration. Then he and Judith Nathan went to Ground Zero—Giuliani wanted it to be the last place he visited before he left.

In the fall of 2002, Giuliani proposed to Nathan during a business trip to Paris. Nathan's emotional support during Giuliani's cancer scare two years earlier had brought the couple closer together, but it was 9/11 that cinched the deal. "We were close already, and then we went through hell together," Giuliani says. He said the experience of working together under such immense pressure gave him a new appreciation for Nathan's knowledge, compassion, and generous spirit. "It was an eye-opener," he says.

In 2003 Giuliani and Nathan exchanged vows in a civil ceremony on the lawn of Gracie Mansion. Mayor Michael

Giuliani and Judith Nathan pose as they arrive for their wedding rehearsal. *(Courtesy of AP Images/Diane Bondareff)*

Bloomberg presided over the ceremony. The four-hundred-person guest list included Yogi Berra, Henry Kissinger, and Donald Trump. Giuliani's son Andrew was the best man.

It wasn't just Giuliani's personal life that took a turn for the better after City Hall. Mayors before Giuliani have left the office defeated by the so-called ungovernable city. John Lindsay, blamed for many of New York's social and financial problems in the 1970s, didn't seek reelection. His successor, Abraham Beame, spent the next four years fending off bankruptcy. His party didn't nominate him for a second term. David Dinkins lost to Giuliani in 1993. "The New York mayoralty," says historian and Giuliani biographer Fred Siegel, "has long been a graveyard for political ambitions,"

Due in large part to his leadership on 9/11, Giuliani's departure from City Hall was an auspicious occasion. "America's Mayor" had become a popular national political figure. In the 2002 congressional election, Giuliani campaigned for Republicans in nineteen states, helping his party expand their majority in the House and regain the Senate. It was a major step for Giuliani to become more partisan. Clearly, the 2008 presidential race was on his mind.

In 2004, Giuliani received a standing ovation at the Republican Convention in New York. His speech secured

Giuliani receives a standing ovation at the 2004 Republican National Convention. *(Courtesy of AP Images/J. Scott Applewhite)*

his place on the national political stage. He made a strong case for George Bush's foreign policy—some said he made a better case than the President had. The *New York Daily News* headline said it all: "America's Mayor Hits a Home Run for W."

After Giuliani helped President Bush defeat Democrat John Kerry, he was considered for a number of prominent posts within Bush's cabinet, including attorney general and secretary of homeland security. But Giuliani, his eye on the presidency, didn't show much interest in subordinate roles.

Giuliani used the opportunity to try to help out his old friend Bernie Kerik. When head of homeland security Tom Ridge announced his retirement, Giuliani recommended that President Bush appoint New York Police Commissioner Kerik. Soon after the President announced the appointment, Kerik revealed that he had failed to pay Social Security taxes for his children's nanny, and withdrew his nomination. It wasn't long before the true scandal surfaced: Kerik had used an apartment near Ground Zero that was intended for rescue workers as a love nest for two women with whom he was having affairs. Giuliani's judgment came further into question when it was discovered that Kerik had not been given a background check before becoming police commissioner. Giuliani had badly damaged his relationship with President Bush, someone who will have a big say in which candidate gets the 2008 Republican nomination.

Instead, he stayed in the private sector as CEO of Giuliani Partners, a top-tier consulting firm. Giuliani's clients ranged from hospitals to horse-racing operations. He advised them on subjects, such as disaster response and security. Many of the "partners" in Giuliani Partners are his long-term friends and associates. Richard Sheirer, a senior vice president, is the former director of the Office of Emergency Management. Thomas Von Essen, a senior vice president, was the city's fire commissioner. Joseph Volpe was served as the Metropolitan Opera's general manager for sixteen years before joining Giuliani Partners.

Giuliani, who once thought that his clerking salary of $11,000 was big time, was at the helm of a company bringing in $100 million a year in revenue. He traveled to speaking engagements around the world, commanding fees of $75,000 and more. In 2002, *Consulting* magazine named him "Consultant of the Year."

In November 2006, Giuliani established a presidential exploratory committee, the first step toward the 2008 race. He traveled around the country, conducting polls and focus groups. In February 2007 he filed a statement of candidacy with the Federal Election Commission. He also started to build a campaign staff. His former chief of staff from the mayor's office, Anthony Carbonetti, become his chief advisor. He hired the former northeast regional director for President Bush's 2004 reelection campaign as his campaign manager. Katie Levinson, communications director for California Governor Arnold Schwarzenegger, also joined Giuliani's staff.

Giuliani continues to fundraise. The contributions he's received so far trail those of four of his major opponents: Republican Mitt Romney and Democrats Hillary Clinton and Barack Obama all have more campaign money. Giuliani's supporters include actors Kelsey Grammer and Adam Sandler. Both have contributed the maximum donations allowed for individuals, $2,100.

In all of his campaign speeches, Giuliani talks about the Iraq War. He says he sides with President Bush, supporting the war and the deployment of more troops. But while the President is sure the war will be a success, Giuliani admits that it may not work out. He suggests that his approach as president will be different—but he hasn't said exactly what his approach would be. He has emphasized in his speeches that the United States needs to look beyond Iraq at the threats posed by Iran, Syria, Pakistan, and Afghanistan.

According to political analysts, Giuliani's vagueness over Iraq is part of a twofold strategy: he can't alienate pro-war voters if he hopes to win the Republican nomination, but in order to win the presidency in the general election he has to appeal to antiwar voters.

It's unclear as to whether or not Giuliani's moderate stance regarding important issues will estrange him from Republican voters. *(Courtesy of AP Images/Mark Lennihan)*

Giuliani's positions on social issues are contradictory as well. He has said that he thinks abortion is wrong, but that he respects a woman's right to choose. He recently went on the record as supporting the Supreme Court's ban on the rare dilation and extraction method of abortion (sometimes called "partial birth" abortion), but in 2000 he said he would vote to protect women's access to that option. Years ago Giuliani said that public funding for abortions for poor women was important, that women should have the resources to choose between abortion and other options. But in a 2007 debate he said that funding is an issue for states to decide, indicating that as president he would not approve federal funding for abortion. Even though his critics and supporters describe him as pro-choice, Giuliani has hinted on at least one occasion that he might help ban all abortion in America—when asked who he would appoint to the Supreme Court if he were President, he answered strict constructionist judges. Strict constructionist is a shorthand that conservatives use to describe judges who would be likely to overturn or limit Roe v. Wade, the 1973 decision that ruled abortion a constitutionally protected right.

As mayor of New York, Giuliani strayed from the conservative base by supporting gun control and speaking out in favor of a licensing system for gun owners that would include mandatory firearms training and background checks. He also lobbied Congress to outlaw semiautomatic assault weapons. When dozens of cities organized a lawsuit against the gun industry, Giuliani was the only Republican mayor to join. As a presidential candidate, Giuliani has changed his tune. He's said he supports individuals' Second Amendment right to bear arms, and he no longer supports a federal ban on assault weapons.

Giuliani's position on gay rights has changed as well, although not as much as some conservatives would like. In 2004 he came out against President Bush's proposed constitutional ban on gay marriage. Giuliani believed the ban was an unnecessary measure, but he doesn't support the legalization of gay marriage. Unlike many Republicans, he does support domestic partnerships that provide same sex couples with some legal benefits.

Giuliani speaks during a fundraiser in this 2007 photo. *(Courtesy of AP Images/Seth Wenig)*

Instead of widening his appeal, it's possible that Giuliani's unconventional positions could alienate voters on both sides of the issues. On the other hand, his views could speak to a growing number of Republican voters who are also ambivalent about social issues and the controversial Iraq War. Voters tend to reward politicians for thinking independently.

Giuliani's challengers for the Republican nomination have opinions that are more in line with the GOP's base. Senator John McCain from Arizona used to have a reputation for bucking his party, but now he is one of President Bush's most staunch supporters in the Iraq War. Mitt Romney, the former governor of Massachusetts, has described himself as unapologetically pro-life.

If Giuliani does win his party's nomination, and New York Senator Hillary Clinton has the same success, the two could face off in the general election. America would get to see a rematch of the contest that never was, when Giuliani dropped out of the 2000 New York Senate race six months before the election. In a nod to his friend and Yankees great Yogi Berra, Giuliani said "it could be déjà vu all over again."

**

At Rudy Giuliani's 1997 inauguration, eighty-eight-year-old Helen Giuliani told reporters that she would one day see her son sworn in as president. She died in 2002—with Giuliani, Judith, Andrew, and Caroline at her bedside—but she would be happy to know that her son is closer than ever to the highest office in the land.

The warm welcome the Republican party gave Giuliani at the 2004 Convention hasn't cooled. Considered too liberal by the far right and too conservative by the far left, Giuliani has a strong appeal for a large number of Americans in the middle. As a Republican who managed to govern a predominantly Democratic city, it's safe to say that Giuliani shouldn't be underestimated.

His political liabilities—the "weirdness factor" of his first marriage, his serial infidelity, his father's criminal past—have been around for a long time and haven't destroyed his career yet. "None of us, at least I don't think any of us, have perfect lives," Giuliani has said. "I can say very credibly to people, 'Judge me by my public performance. Whatever mistakes I've made in my personal life, I made, I'm sorry for them.'"

Giuliani's public performance has had highs and lows, but his ambition, discipline, courage, and tireless dedication have been consistent. He's had the presidency in his sights for a long time, so one thing's for sure: Giuliani, a student at heart, has been busy preparing, studying, analyzing, and strategizing. If he does get the Republican nomination, he'll be a formidable opponent.

Timeline

1944 Born Rudolph William Louis Giuliani III in
Brooklyn, New York, on May 28.

1951 Moves to Long Island.

**1951
–1957** Attends St. Anne's, a local Catholic school.

**1957
–1961** Attends Bishop Loughlin Memorial High School.

1961 Attends Manhattan College in Riverdale,
–1965 The Bronx, majoring in political science and
philosophy.

1965 Attends New York University School of Law in
–1968 Manhattan, graduating cum laude with a Doctor
of Jurisprudence.

1968 Marries his second cousin, Regina Peruggi.

1968 Clerks for Judge Lloyd F. MacMahon, United States
–1970 District Court Judge for the Southern District of
New York.

1970 Joins the Office of the U.S. Attorney
in the Southern District of New York.

1975 Recruited to Washington, D.C., as associate

deputy attorney general in the United States
Department of Justice.

1977   Returns to New York to practice law at Patterson,
-1981   Belknap, Webb & Tyler.

1981   Father, Harold, dies of prostate cancer; appointed U.S.
        associate attorney general by President Ronald
        Reagan.

1982   Divorces Regina Peruggi; Catholic Church grants an
        annulment the following year.

1983   Becomes an executive U.S. attorney for the Southern
        District of New York.

1984   Marries Donna Hanover.

1986   Son Andrew born.

1989   Daughter Caroline born; loses his first race for
        mayor by the closest margin in New York City's
        history.

1993   Elected the 107th mayor of New York City, the first
        Republican to hold the post in twenty years.

1997   Reelected to a second term.

2000   Diagnosed with prostate cancer; withdraws from
        the Senate race and undergoes months of radiation
        treatment.

2001 Show of leadership on 9/11 transforms him into a national hero.

2002 Presented Ronald Reagan Presidential Freedom Award by former first lady Nancy Reagan; receives honorary knighthood from Queen Elizabeth II; divorces Donna Hanover; best-selling book *Leadership* is published; launches Giuliani Partners, LLC, a management consulting firm.

2003 Marries Judith Nathan.

2007 Announces his candidacy for president in the 2008 race.

Sources

CHAPTER ONE: Yankee Fan

p. 11, "I'm never going to have . . ." Deborah Hart Strober and Gerald S. Strober, *Giuliani: Flawed or Flawless? The Oral Biography* (Hoboken, NJ: John Wiley & Sons, Inc., 2007), 3.

p. 13, "If you can survive as . . ." Ibid., 16.

p. 15, "your savage," Wayne Barrett, *Rudy!: An Investigative Biography of Rudolph Giuliani* (New York: Basic Books, 2000), 14.

p. 16, "Instead of a class . . ." Rudolph W. Giuliani, *Leadership* (New York: Miramax Books, 2002), 285.

p. 17, "I knew parts of it . . ." Eric Pooley, "Mayor of the World," *Time*, December 31, 2001.

p. 18, "My father compensated through me . . ." Ibid.

p. 18, "His parents brought him up . . ." Ibid.

p. 18, "It's a great privilege to . . ." Ibid.

p. 18, "As a Yankees fan growing . . ." Giuliani, *Leadership*, 265-266.

p. 19, "Never be a bully." Ibid., 269.

p. 19, "New York produces tough kids . . ." Strober and Strober, *Giuliani: Flawed or Flawless? The Oral Biography*, 22.

p. 20, "I grew up with uniforms . . ." Pooley, "Mayor of the World."

p. 20, "Rudy was right . . ." Barry Bearak and Ian Fisher. "Race for City Hall: The Republican Candidate; A Mercurial Mayor's Confident Journey," *New York Times*, October 19, 1997.

p. 20, "oddball," Bearak and Fisher, "Race for City Hall: The Republican Candidate; A Mercurial Mayor's Confident Journey."

p. 21, "Whatever he got into . . ." Strober and Strober, *Giuliani: Flawed or Flawless? The Oral Biography*, 25.

p. 21, "Giuliani was always around . . ." Pooley, "Mayor of the World."

p. 24, "I think she had . . ." Barrett, *Rudy!: An Investigative Biography of Rudolph Giuliani*, 44.

p. 25, "Good luck in seminary," Richard Stengel, "The Passionate Prosecutor U.S." *Time*, June 24, 2001.

p. 25, "I realized I had . . ." Giuliani, *Leadership*, 172-173.

p. 25, "The Giulianis wanted grandchildren," Bearak and Fisher, "Race for City Hall: The Republican Candidate; A Mercurial Mayor's Confident Journey."

p. 26, "to be the first Italian . . ." Barrett, *Rudy!: An Investigative Biography of Rudolph Giuliani*, 52.

p. 27, "Quite a family affair!" Ibid., 54.

p. 27, "My son is very affectionate . . ." Ibid.

CHAPTER TWO: Crime Buster

p. 28, "I thought I was rich," Giuliani, *Leadership*, 229.

p. 29, "It wasn't until I understood . . ." Ibid., 230.

p. 29, "If Giuliani is the nominee . . ." Geoffrey Gray, "Rudy and Nam," *New York*, April 23, 2007.

p. 29, "There's a big gap . . ." Giuliani, *Leadership*, 233.

p. 30-31, "The U.S. Attorney's office in . . ." Ibid., 120.

p. 31-32, "I tried the most difficult . . ." Ibid., 212.

p. 32, "I didn't even know what . . ." Ibid., 181.

p. 32, "Tyler was very good under . . ." Barrett, *Rudy!: An Investigative Biography of Rudolph Giuliani*, 92.

p. 33, "We expected that Rudy would . . ." Strober and Strober, *Giuliani: Flawed or Flawless? The Oral Biography*, 39.

p. 35-36, "The image I had . . ." Giuliani, *Leadership*, 182.

p. 39, "Being the U.S. attorney was . . ." Strober and Strober, *Giuliani: Flawed or Flawless? The Oral Biography*, 41.

p. 40-41, "I think the fact that . . ." Ibid., 46.

p. 41, "It's about time law enforcement . . ." Barrett, *Rudy!: An Investigative Biography of Rudolph Giuliani*, 146.

p. 41, "I want to send . . ." Ibid., 148.

p. 41, "A lot of people around . . ." Ibid.

p. 42, "This isn't an invitation to . . ." Ibid., 159.

p. 42, "Only the little people . . ." Associated Press, "Maid Testifies Helmsley Denied Paying Taxes: Says She Told Her 'Only the Little People Pay,'" *New York Times*, July 12 1989.

p. 43, "In a tarnished, soulless city . . ." Barrett, *Rudy!: An Investigative Biography of Rudolph Giuliani*, 162.

p. 43, "Every time the FBI . . ." Ibid., 161.

CHAPTER THREE: The Giuliani Revolution

p. 44, "a candidate in search of . . ." Richard J. Meislin, "Scandal In City Bringing Added Fame To Giuliani," *New York Times*, April 13, 1986.

p. 44-45, "This is the city . . ." Barrett, *Rudy!: An Investigative Biography of Rudolph Giuliani*, 190.

p. 47, "As I waited for . . ." Giuliani, *Leadership*, 272.

p. 47, "a crusading Batman," Catherine S. Manegold, "The 1993 Elections: Man in the News; A Road of

Many Turns, an End Triumphant: Rudolph William Giuliani," *New York Times*, November 3, 1993.

p. 47, "wooden," Barrett, *Rudy!: An Investigative Biography of Rudolph Giuliani*, 210.

p. 47, "robotic," Ibid.

p. 48, "If he held up . . ." Ibid.

p. 49, "If I were the mayor . . ." Giuliani, *Leadership*, 56.

p. 49, "It was almost like being . . ." Ibid., 57.

p. 49, "vulnerability report," Howard Kurtz, "In 1993 Memo, Giuliani Staff Gave Harsh Assessment of Flaws," *Washington Post*, February 14, 2007.

p. 50, "weirdness factor," Ibid.

p. 51, "Nobody, no ethnic, religious . . ." Barrett, *Rudy!: An Investigative Biography of Rudolph Giuliani*, 286.

p. 52, "Broken Windows," Giuliani, *Leadership*, 47.

p. 54, "probably the most powerful control . . ." Ibid., 75.

p. 55, "He's not a racist . . ." Strober and Strober, *Giuliani: Flawed or Flawless? The Oral Biography*, 150.

p. 59, "Before September 11, there were . . ." Giuliani, *Leadership*, 63.

CHAPTER FOUR: Blame and Brutality

p. 60, "possibly the only good thing . . ." Barrett, *Rudy!: An Investigative Biography of Rudolph Giuliani*, 10.

p. 62, "an altar boy," Eric Lipton, "Giuliani Cites Criminal Past Of Slain Man," *New York Times*, March 20, 2000.

p. 62-63, "There's a new category . . ." Strober and Strober, *Giuliani: Flawed or Flawless? The Oral Biography*, 202.

p. 65, "sick stuff," Robert D. McFadden, "Disputed Madonna Painting In Brooklyn Show Is Defaced," *New York Times*, December 17, 1999.

p. 67, "Listening tour," Jonathan P. Hicks, "Unusual Mix
of Political Methods Shapes Mrs. Clinton's Tour," *New
York Times*, August 9, 1999.

p. 68, "A very good friend," Elisabeth Bumiller,
"Mayor Acknowledges 'Very Good Friend,'" *New
York Times*, May 4, 2000.

p. 68-69, "Giuliani is once again expressing . . ." Pooley,
"Mayor of the World."

p. 69, "For several years . . . " Elisabeth Bumiller, "The
Mayor's Separation: The Overview; Giuliani and His
Wife of 16 Years are Separating," *New York Times*,
May 11, 2000.

p. 69-70, "Because I've been in public . . ." "The Mayor's
Decision; Excerpts From Giuliani's Remarks on Decision
to Withdraw," *New York Times*, May 20, 2000.

p. 70, "The reason . . . " Ibid.

p. 70, "I hope he's closer . . ." Ibid.

CHAPTER FIVE: September 11

p. 73, "It had to be even . . ." Giuliani, *Leadership*, 5.

p. 74, "We're in unchartered waters now," Ibid., 7.

p. 75, "God bless you," Ibid., 8.

p. 77, "It's coming down—everybody down!" Ibid., 11.

p. 78, "It's terrible out there . . ." Amanda Ripley,
"We're Under Attack," *Time*, December 23, 2001.

p. 79, "If I have to die . . ." Ibid.

p. 79, "We are kind of like . . ." Ibid.

p. 82, "I decided right away not . . ." Giuliani,
Leadership, 25.

p. 82, "Hatred, prejudice, and anger . . ." Fred Siegel, *The
Prince of the City: Giuliani, New York and the Genius
of American Life* (New York: Encounter Books,
2005), 306.

p. 82, "It's going to be a . . ." Ripley, "We're Under Attack."

p. 83, "Now it was our turn . . ." Giuliani, *Leadership*, 26.

CHAPTER SIX: America's Mayor

p. 84, "The question, among critics . . ." Catherine S. Manegold, "The 1993 Elections: Man in the News; A Road of Many Turns, an End Triumphant: Rudolph William Giuliani," *New York Times*, November 3, 1993.

p. 85, "I was mayor . . ." Wayne Barrett and Dan Collins, "Rudy's Grand Illusion," *Village Voice*, August 29, 2006.

p. 90-91, "A surprising number of them . . ." Giuliani, *Leadership*, 376.

p. 92, "New York is still here . . ." Stephen Rodrick, "Rudy Tuesday," *New York*, March 5, 2007.

p. 92, "In a crisis you have . . ." Pooley, "Mayor of the World."

p. 93, "What Giuliani succeeded in doing . . ." Ibid.

p. 94, "blood, toil, tears, and sweat," Ibid.

CHAPTER SEVEN: 20/20 Hindsight

p. 96, "The emergency response . . ." National Commission on Terrorist Attacks, *The 9/11 Commission Report: Final Report of the National Commission on Terrorist Attacks Upon the United States* (New York: W.W. Norton & Company), 2004.

p. 99, "The last thing the city . . ." Giuliani, *Leadership*, 373.

p. 99-100, "Four more years, four more . . ." Siegel, "The Prince of the City: Giuliani, New York and the Genius of American Life," 309.

CHAPTER EIGHT: Life After City Hall

p. 102, "We were close already . . ." Associated Press, "Giuliani To Wed At Gracie Mansion," *CBS News*, April 25, 2003.

p. 102, "It was an eye-opener," Giuliani, *Leadership*, 356.

p. 103-104, "The New York mayoralty has . . ." Siegel, "The Prince of the City: Giuliani, New York and the Genius of American Life," 330-331.

p. 104, "America's Mayor," Ibid., 327.

p. 105, "America's Mayor Hits a Home . . ." Ibid., 328.

p. 110, "It's deja vu all over . . ." Maggie Haberman, "Hill and Rudy on Road to Rematch," *New York Post*, December 10, 2006.

p. 111, "weirdness factor," Howard Kurtz, "In 1993 Memo, Giuliani Staff Gave Harsh Assessment of Flaws."

p. 111, "None of us, at least . . ." Associate Press, "Giuliani, wife discuss White House roles," *MSNBC.com*, March 29, 2007.

Bibliography

Associated Press. "Giuliani To Wed At Gracie Mansion."
CBSNews.com, April 25, 2003.
———. "Giuliani, wife discuss White House roles."
MSNBC.com, March 29, 2007.
———. "Maid Testifies Helmsley Denied Paying Taxes:
Says She Told Her 'Only the Little People Pay.'" *New
York Times*, July 12 1989.
BBC News. "Profile: Michael Bloomberg." August 27, 2004.
Barrett, Wayne. *Rudy!: An Investigative Biography of
Rudolph Giuliani*. New York: Basic Books, 2000.
Barrett, Wayne, and Dan Collins. "Rudy's Grand
Illusion." *Village Voice*, August 29, 2006.
Bearak, Barry, and Ian Fisher. "Race for City Hall: The
Republican Candidate; A Mercurial Mayor's
Confident Journey." *New York Times*, October 19, 1997.
Brenner, Marie. "Incident in the 70th Precinct." *Vanity
Fair*, December 1997.

Bull, Chris. "Cutting It Close." *Advocate*, June 14, 1994.

———. "The Tolerant Bully." *Advocate*, June 28, 1994.

Bumiller, Elisabeth. "The Mayor's Decision: The Overview; Cancer Is Concern." *New York Times*, May 20, 2000.

Cooper, Michael. "Helen Giuliani, 92, Mother of Former New York Mayor." *New York Times*, September 9, 2002.

———. "Mayor's Response to a Fatal Police Shooting a Departure From His Predecessors'." *New York Times*, January 26, 2004.

Giuliani, Rudolph W. *Leadership*. New York: Miramax Books, 2002.

———. "The Mayor's Decision; Excerpts From Giuliani's Remarks on Decision to Withdraw." *New York Times*, May 20, 200

Gordon, Craig. "Rudy: Brooklyn loyalty no slight to Long Island." *Newsday Long Island*, April 11, 2007.

Gray, Geoffrey. "Rudy and 'Nam." *New York*, April 23, 2007.

Keen, Judy. "Pool Report." *USA Today*, September 11, 2001.

Kurtz, Howard. "In 1993 Memo, Giuliani Staff Gave Harsh Assessment of Flaws." *Washington Post*, February 14, 2007.

Lemonick, Michael D. "Deadly Delivery." *Time*, October 22, 2001.

Leonard, Devin. "Can Rudy Giuliani tame the beast within?" *New York Observer*, May 10, 1999.

Lipton, Eric. "Giuliani Cites Criminal Past Of Slain Man." *New York Times*, March 20, 2000.

Lyall, Sarah. "In London, Giuliani Is Honorary Knight but Bona Fide Hero." *New York Times*, February 14, 2002.

Manegold, Catherine S. "The 1993 Elections: Man in the News; A Road of Many Turns, an End Triumphant: Rudolph William Giuliani." *New York Times*, November 3, 1993.

McFadden, Robert D. "Disputed Madonna Painting In Brooklyn Show Is Defaced." *New York Times*, December 17, 1999.

Meislin, Richard J. "Scandal In City Bringing Added Fame To Giuliani." *New York Times*, April 13, 1986.

National Commission on Terrorist Attacks. *The 9/11 Commission Report: Final Report of the National Commission on Terrorist Attacks Upon the United States.* New York: W. W. Norton & Company, 2004.

Pooley, Eric. "Mayor of the World." *Time*, December 31, 2001.

Price, Diana. "Judith Giuliani: A Caregiver's Perspective." *Women & Cancer*, Winter 2006.

Quinnipiac University. "Mayor's Approval Bounces Back To 18-Month High, Quinnipiac University Poll Finds; High Marks On Crime, Low Marks On Education, Race." Hamden, CT: June 14, 2000.

Richardson, Lynda. "Public Lives; A Scholarly Fund-Raiser's Stroll to the Park." *New York Times*, May 4, 2001.

Ripley, Amanda. "We're Under Attack." *Time*, December 23, 2001.

Robbins, Tom. "An Anniversary: The Manes Scandals." *Village Voice*, January 10, 2006.

Rodrick, Stephen. "Rudy Tuesday," *New York*, March 5, 2007.

Schwartzman, Paul. "Rudy's Rules." *Playboy*, March 1999.

Siegel, Fred. *The Prince of the City: Giuliani, New York and the Genius of American Life*, New York: Encounter Books, 2005.

Stengel, Richard. "The Passionate Prosecutor U.S." *Time*, June 24, 2001.

Strober, Deborah Hart, and Gerald S. Strober. *Giuliani:*

Flawed or Flawless? The Oral Biography. Hoboken, NJ: John Wiley & Sons, Inc., 2007.

Weisner, Benjamin. "Judge Rejects Giuliani's Attempt To Kill Bus Ads Using His Name." *New York Times,* December 2, 1997.

Winerip, Michael. "High Profile Prosecutor." *New York Times,* June 9, 1985.

Web sites

http://www.joinrudy2008.com
Rudy Giuliani's official campaign site.

http://www.giulianipartners.com
The online home of Rudy Giuliani's management consulting firm.

http://giulianiblog.blogspot.com
A blog following Giuliani's campaign developments.

http://www.time.com/time/poy2001
The online profile of *Time* news magazine's 2001 Person of the Year, Rudy Giuliani.

Index

Political Profiles